SHAPE OF EXTINCTION

ASEMANA
BOOKS

SHAPE OF EXTINCTION

Poems by
Bijan Jalali

Translated from the Persian
by Adeeba Shahid Talukder and Aria Fani
Preface by Domenico Ingenito
Critical introduction by Aria Fani
Cover illustration & artwork by Amelia Ossorio

ASEMANA BOOKS

Toronto, Canada
First Edition
© 2025 by Asemana Books

ALL RIGHTS RESERVED.
No part of this book may be reproduced or transmitted in any form or by any means, electronic or mechanical, including photocopying, recording, or by any information storage and retrieval system, without prior written permission from the publisher, except for the inclusion of brief quotations in a review.

Published by ASEMANA BOOKS

ISBN: 978-1-0690210-8-3

Book Design: Asemana Books

Cover illustration & artwork: Amelia Ossorio
Cover design: Caro Reed-Ferrara

To find out more about our authors and books visit: www.asemanabooks.ca

ASEMANA BOOKS

For Abbu
who is in every poem
—Adeeba

To Chana Kronfeld
for the love of poetry
—Aria

Contents

The Numbness of Non-Existence: Translating Jalali's *Ineffable Sorrow* and its Transformative Transitions, Domenico A. Ingenito...........................ix

Poems in Persian and English...........................43

In Quiet Revolt: The Poetic Legacy of Bijan Jalali, Aria Fani...........................167

Acknowledgements...........................225

Behind the Words and Images...........................226

The Numbness of Non-Existence: Translating Jalali's *Ineffable Sorrow* and its Transformative Transitions

Domenico A. Ingenito

Or the Inexplicable End of Precious Bonds

Reading Bijan Jalali's poetry feels like listening to distant words that a dear friend whispers into your ear late at night. You wake up and realize that your friend was never there next to you; you fail to recognize their identity in the dream, and nothing remains of their words of affectionate wisdom but a faint echo that you'll never be able to recall. You go on with your daily tasks, and nothing tangible stays with you except the numbing presence of some sort of hollowness, or an inexplicable betrayal of unconditional care and affection in its purest manifestation—not a true form of lacking, but the experience of not knowing what went amiss. Not just pain, but the ellipsis that follows the end of things that never were:

ineffable sorrow…[1]

The first time I heard about Bijan Jalali's life and poetry, I was living in Tehran, completing my doctoral dissertation on the medieval Persian poet Hafez of Shiraz. I was in my mid-twenties, and life in Iran felt incredibly exciting for an Italian student who had

---

1

chosen Tehran as his second home. My morning sessions at the University of Tehran were intensely bittersweet, dazzlingly rich, and plainly joyful. After class, my friends and I would go to the bustling Enqelab street to compulsively buy books that we pretended were absolutely indispensable for our academic future. In those chaotic streets that reminded me of my hometown, Naples, I refined the art of reading medieval Persian poetry while walking and simultaneously avoiding cars and scooters. My roommates used to host a film club every Wednesday night. Poets, filmmakers, producers, photographers and artists of all backgrounds would join us, keeping our conversations going until past midnight. I was living with my friend N. (and a bunch of other people, as it was never clear who *actually* lived there with us), and she would make tea and eggs for us every morning. I would read her lines from unpopular poets (such as Jāmi) or obscure authors (think of Owhadi of Maraghe) while we moistened our tiny and impossibly dry Bahman cigarettes by holding them just above our steamy teacups.

One day, probably in April 2008, a poet friend took me to the legendary Shuka Café on the then up-and-coming Gandhi Street. Before sitting down (I recall that both the chairs and the table were scarlet red), my friend pointed to the wall behind the coffee bar to show me a drawing depicting a middle-aged man with angel-like wings. The entire section of the wall was dedicated to Bijan Jalali. After recognizing my friend, the café owner approached us: "Yes, he was an angel. He was not even interested in women or romantic relationships." They showed me one of his poetry collections. I was immediately struck by the epigrammatic style of Jalali's minimalist compositions. At the same time, the café owner's comment made me think of the queer dimensions of medieval Persian poetry; an aspect that, at the time, I believed seldom surfaced in the context of contemporary Iran's heteronormative literary canon (Ingenito, 2020). I asked the owner to tell us more about Jalali. I don't recall his exact words, but the expression *bi-hessi*—numbness—stayed with me. He said that he had never met a person so consumed by the absolute *struggle of numbness*.

Figure 1: The cover of *Yaddasht'ha-ye yek qahve'chi* (Tehran: Giv, 2000), penned by Yar'ali Purmoqadam, the celebrated playwright and the beloved owner of Shuka Café

Friendship in Translation

Weeks later, I started translating some of Jalali's poems into Italian. I was baffled by the paradoxical difficulty of translating texts that seem untranslatable precisely because of their formal simplicity. When encountering such disarmingly simple poems, even the most experienced translator might have to resist the urge to beautify her versions so as not to overshadow the original text's apparent formal poverty. I was young and inexperienced. My translations read as a constant attempt at beautifying Jalali's poems. A photographer friend, Mohammadreza Mirzaei, and I put together a book proposal in which we combined my translations with one of his most recent photographic series, *Didārhā / Gli Incontri* (*The Encounters*). We never published the book, mainly because I became increasingly aware of the mindfulness that such delicate fragments required when forced into another language. I still keep digital copies of those images and the highly contrasted silhouettes of the people they portray—ghostly presences that resemble holograms of a hologram, or black-and-white reflections of the mysterious human beings described by Adolfo Bioy Casares in *Morel's Invention*.

I have been thinking about Jalali's existential numbness and his ghostly lines for almost twenty years. Only months ago, when my dear friend Aria Fani shared the manuscript of this book, did I finally understand what the café owner meant that day. Almost immediately, I said to myself that Jalali's poetry has finally found its ideal translators: consummate poet, Adeeba Shahid Talukder and, of course, Aria himself.

In recent years, friends have described Aria Fani as the embodiment of *adab*—that is, the Persian way of combining the ethics of friendship with the aesthetic rigor that intellectual labor demands. When we first met back in 2014, Aria was roughly the same age I was when I had my first encounter with Jalali's poetry. We were so absorbed in our nocturnal peripatetic conversation in the streets of Washington D.C., that we had to keep watching our steps to make sure we didn't leave our other friends behind. Having recently moved to the US from Italy by way of Oxford, I was navigating the existential complexity of living and working *with and through* two languages, English and Persian, that I had learned later in life, while progressively losing touch with my mother tongue. That night, Aria shared thoughts about the first article I ever published, a short piece critiquing Italian and French translations of Hafez's poetry (Ingenito, 2009). As a junior scholar, I was deeply moved by the fact that an engaging PhD student from Berkeley had relied on his fluency in Spanish in order to access one of my juvenile pieces of academic writing in Italian.

Talking with Aria about translation and the false myth of the untranslatability of poetic texts renewed my interest in the socio-political aspects of the practice of transferring poetry across linguistic and cultural contexts. Years later, Aria published his own brilliant take on the problem of untranslatability of Persian poems (Fani, 2020). We recognized in each other the desire of experiencing translation as an active critique of national and linguistic identities and as a creative tool for understanding how cultural nationalisms lead to social injustice within and beyond the boundaries of the academic space. We never addressed it in these terms explicitly, but I believe that the numbness Jalali reportedly experienced throughout his life was one of the unspoken aspects of how Aria and I developed an emotionally vulnerable engagement with the practice and theory of translation. It is a sensation that reveals the in-between areas—the soft spots—where we, as friends and colleagues, meet when facing the ever-changing challenges of translating from, to, and through Persian texts, along with the permanent feeling of displacement that this practice brings about.

Resisting Visibility

Vulnerability and dislocation are the affective response that ethically aware translators like Adeeba Talukder and Aria Fani have had to confront when reconstructing the disarming simplicity of Jalali's style:

how much of a poet
must one be

to see a flower
to recite a flower

Translating simplicity and repetition without trying to hystericize Jalali's original text—to make it sound more evocative than it is, for instance—reveals a key point of the author's poetics: ways of saying, of *seeing* (as John Berger would say), constitute for Jalali the primary *act* of poetry. The implication of this seemingly self-explanatory truth is that the things of the world cannot be truly seen and, as a consequence, cannot be pronounced: they cannot even exist without poetry's *act*. From this perspective, non-existence—of which death is but a contingent manifestation—intersects with the very destiny of poetry as a relentless economy of resistance and abandonment that shapes the relationship between Being and Language. "How much / of a poet / must one be," or: how *much* must one *be*, especially when realizing that non-being could well constitute the foundation of being as an illusionary condition?

A few years ago, when I was still unaware of the health condition that would eventually lead him to his untimely demise, I shared with my dear colleague and friend, Prof. Franklin Lewis, my translation of a few lines composed by the Portuguese poet Herberto Helder: "We all touch each other / like trees amidst / an underground forest / we are a reflection of the dead: / the world is not real; / for us to cope with this / without dying of fear, / words, only words." Frank replied immediately, citing the first lines of Helder's poem: "It is indeed a poetic armor for the human condition: *É preciso criar palavras, sons, palavras vivas, obscuras, terríveis*" ("Húmus," Helder, 1990). Generations of scholars and translators come and go. Regardless of the structures that surround the dull technocratic and administrative violence of all academic spaces, intellectual communities ought to cling to the power of language to overcome the violence of non-existence, which ultimately leads to the possibility of relinquishing the fear of death that dramatizes our speaking existences. The necessity of creating "terrible" words, "living" words, animates Jalali's poetic quest. His is an invisible act which only translators as sensitive as Aria and Adeeba can fully disclose. The simplicity of these texts is what makes the translator's mandate particularly urgent— vital, dare I say.

Translating difficult poets is an easy task, especially for translators who aim to challenge the normatively sexist logic of fidelity to the original text. If translating poetry is an act of creative re-composition, stylistically intricate, semantically dense, or symbolically open poems can be freely rendered in another language through what translators refer to as the "compensation principle" (Osimo, 2011). The idea behind this principle is that, as Henry Meschonnic once provocatively argued, a good translation ought to render not only what the original text *says* but also what the text *does*—the *performance* it brings about, the *event* it generates, within and beyond History's contingencies (Meschonnic, 2011, p. 69). Given poetry's obsessive reliance on form (including rhythm, figures of style, patterns of sound, etc.) for the emergence of meaning as an act of embodiment (through recitation, affective responses, mnemonic and imaginative activation, etc.), the event that a given poem produces—its act of *doing* rather than merely *saying*—stems from a myriad of variables whose complex architectural structures defy the myth of pure correspondence between languages. If loss of meaning and affect is assumed from the outset—not only because of the intrinsic specificity of each poetic text in its relationship with the literary and linguistic system to which it belongs—then translating poetry should be regarded as an act of approximative compensation.

The apparently colloquial simplicity of Jalali's poetry defies the radical translator's creative act and resists the notion of an absolute difference between original and translated texts (Berman, 1999). Against all contemporary critical postures on the ethics of translation, Jalali's texts resist the translator's visibility and instead call for their *invisibility* (Venuti, 2008).

These poems seem to desire to be translated by themselves or, even worse, through the alienating blindness of ChatGPT. Fani and Talukder's translations resist this resistance in the finest of fashions, never shying away from following the text in its minimalistic literal forms and meanings, while asserting the translator's visibility to the extent that their versions are both literally close to the original and poetically independent from it.

The World's Sensory Excess and the Numbing Feeling of *No*thingness

A translation that is simultaneously literal and artistically autonomous is a political act of resistance. It brings to the fore both the translator's dignity as a visible interpreter of Otherness and the author of a given text as a concrete historical possibility that transcends time's contingencies and the foreclosures of meaning. By doing so, meaning happens over and over again as an act of defiance that simultaneously celebrates and overcomes the original text and speaks in new and unpredictable ways to the crises of the present time as well as the fundamentally critical ways we experience our being in the world. Through this approach, translations expose their own vibrant fragility, their power to bring forth poetry's mandate (Miglio, 2005). Such translations cease to be mere versions dependent on original forms: they become political events and agents of transformation.

Approaching translation as a catalyst for transformation is an exercise in transparent opacity. Translations mimic the numbing transparency of selfhood: we are who we are, yet we contain multitudes (à la Whitman) that no "are" can fully explain. Reworking the text in a different linguistic texture may force us to approach the original poem as if it were an obscure yet fragrant matter (think of *'anbar*, ambergris) ready to be deciphered. We translate the text because of its supposed opacity, the opacity that envelops the mystery of Otherness. At the same time, perceiving translation as an act of embodiment urges us to think about how to impersonate the presence of the original author: how are we to *become* the creative *other* and let them speak our language through a language we transfix on their behalf? Ultimately, we want to extract secrets from the Other, in order to make *it* intelligible to others. But what if the other, textualized or embodied, living or dead, has no secrets in the first place? What if the "secret" belongs to a different realm of being, as Jalali suggests?

i have no secrets
i just retell
the secret of the blank page

In Persian poetry, the emergence of a secret leads readers towards medieval mysticism and the presence of the *ʿālam-e ghayb*, the invisible realm (Ingenito, 2020, pp. 338–341). Attempts to express linguistically a "concealed secret" (*rāz-e penhān*) abound in the poetry of Sufism-inspired authors such as Rumi and Hafez, as well as esoteric poets such as Nezami. But the truth Jalali conveys here is not related to mysticism alone, as it involves a centuries-long conversation on medieval Persian poetics: the possibility of poetic speech is a mystery that is intrinsic to the blank state of things and their suspended possibility of existence. Poetry retells the impossible presence of things and their absolute detachment from meaning, which discloses itself only when things are no longer present, or not felt, or yet to become. The Aristotelian dimension of Medieval Persian poetry, as Justine Landau teaches us, addresses the contingent linguistic presence of what does not exist but which *might* be possible (Landau, 2013; Ingenito, forthcoming).

The goal of medieval lyric texts (*ghazal*s) and odes (*qaside*s) is to transform external reality rather than to mimic it. Things are captured in their idealized becoming. The idea of poetry as a linguistic reflection of external and biographical events began to appear only at the end of the medieval period, often in conjunction with early modern approaches to mimesis and rhetorically feigned intimacy (such as the so-called "incidentalist" school, or *maktab-e voquʿ-guʾi*) (Losensky,

1998). During the 19th century, intellectual and aesthetic negotiations between Iranian (and Afghan) reflections on canon formation and an underlying quest for literary renewal—inspired by both European models and earlier stages of Persian court poetry—accelerated the emergence of a peculiarly Iranian literary modernity (Ahmed, 2012; Sonboldel, 2024; Fani, 2017; Fani, 2024). It is important to highlight that, in the context of 19th- and early 20th-century Iran, the European romantic models that inspired important strands of the emerging modernist movement had already been highly Persianized by at least two centuries of mutual exchanges (Javadi, 2005; Ingenito and Miglio, 2013; Hartley, 2024). Therefore, the anachronistically Romantic emphasis on the necessity of expressing one's innermost feelings which characterized the poetics of authors such as Nimā Yushij, Fereydun Tavallali, and Forugh Farrokhzad between the 1920s and the 1950s derived from an idiosyncratic Iranian appropriation of European aesthetic models that had already absorbed important aspects of the lyric, didactic, and mystical dimensions of medieval Persian poetry.

Iran's post-Romantic mainstream poetics presents a strong idea of subjectivity as a possibility of language to capture the encounter between personal emotions and the unbearable presence of the world against the poet's psyche and body. Despite key stylistic differences that separate them, poets such as Forugh

Farrokhzad, Ahmad Shamlu, Sohrab Sepehri, and Nader Naderpur rely heavily on the relationship between senses and affect as a means of forcing poetic language against an external reality that demands to be constantly accounted for. Their texts stage the response of lyric subjectivity to an excess of worldly perceptions. Through this process, language turns into a physical articulation that constantly adds new layers of epidermic (sensory or embodied) experience to the experience of the world.

Rather than confronting the experience of sensory excess, the numbing de-sensorialization of Jalali's simple fragments portrays the very impossibility of experiencing the world as an object of experience. Dangerously positioned between the poetic and the non-poetic, Jalali's texts exist in a space where the absence of experience—an absence of *feeling*—compromises subjective self-reflection itself. The lyric *I*, the persona that speaks in his poems, appears as a shell that utters the devastating silence inhabiting the unreachable nature of reality. From the silent vantage point of this numbness, the external world does not truly exist. Instead, it appears as an infinite series of mediated possibilities of being which, like the misleadingly countless layers of an onion, contain nothing at their core. This nothingness—the realization that the Real (both as a mystical myth of Persian Sufi thought, *haqiqat*, and as the Lacanian "Thing" that escapes symbolization) is not only inaccessible but also non-existent—inhabits language itself and, as a consequence, it projects value onto the void that constitutes silence. In fact, for Jalali *non-existence*, as opposed to the negative teleology of *inexistence*, constitutes the core of poetic experience and, as such, the only true experience that human beings can attest to.

Poetics of Silence and Extinction Beyond the Unspeakable: Speaking the *Non-Speakable*

Poetic speech is a temporary stand-in for the absolute silence that frames the texture of reality. It escapes all possibility of expression, for it undermines the very value of expression itself:

when reality
is so unspeakable

one must resort to silence
                      or to verse

Talukder and Fani's choice of translating the Persian adjective *nā-goftani* as "unspeakable" reflects both the pain and the irreducible failure to understand the reality that the Jalali's lyric subject faces when trying to articulate the meaning of things. The mystical substratum of this unspeakable is undeniable, as it derives from the mystery of the invisible realm which, in medieval Persian Sufism, escapes verbal and intellectual apprehension. At the same time, it addresses the impossibility of linguistic articulation that follows the traumatic exposure to horrific events, oppressive tyranny, social injustices, and devastation. Yet, this *nā-goftani* also reveals a deeper form of impossibility of articulation, which could be translated as the "non-speakable." It signifies the ontological absence of meaning —one capable of erasing even meaninglessness itself. Faced with the non-speakable nature of reality, the shell of the *I* dissolves into an impersonal voice ("one must," which renders the subject-less verb, *bāyad*) that can no longer feel and, as a consequence, submits itself to the numbness of silence, the numbness of poetry.

If authors such as Theodor Adorno, Paul Celan, Primo Levi, and Salvatore Quasimodo, grappled with the unspeakable possibilities of poetry after the horrors of the Holocaust, Jalali's non-speakable correspondence between silence and poetry attests to late-capitalist logic and the ontological erasure that characterizes events such as the numbing spectacularization of the Palestinian genocide, the Iranian regime's banal bureaucratization of the sacred sphere for repressive ends, and the devastatingly repressive algorithmic governance of Trump-Musk's dehumanizing global policies of meaninglessness. The numbing effects of genocidal and algorithmic terror, which feed each other into a constant loop of voicelessness and permanent lack of human agency, erode psychological drives from within the subject, including the death drive itself. The encounter between the unspeakable and the non-speakable annihilates the subject's death drive along with the libidinal forces that would normally guide the poet's quest for experience. Drive-less death, for Jalali, is the beginning and the end of poetry, for poetry stands where death does not mean anything but itself:

i have arrived at
my poetry's root:
              death
i bury my verse
      at its feet

This dimension denies both the reality principle and the pleasure principle, thus reconfiguring desire not as a response to lack and erasure, but as a linguistic possibility that fails to meet experience. In Jalali's poetry, the counterpart to the desire to be alive is not the desire to die, but a desire not to exist. In the poem that inspired the title of this book, Jalali expresses negative desire ("i wish to stop existing") as a different shape that death can take ("i wish to die a novel death")—that is, the desire to become *nist*, "non-existent," rather than to experience biological death.

The title, *Shape of Extinction*, captures the double articulation of *nisti*—that is, non-existence *and* extinction—in the forms of reality and destiny. On the one hand, the things of the world do not truly exist. On the other hand, the poet's perception of this non-existence, which structures experience and reveals its mediated nature, announces the end of things as we know them, or as we hope them to subsist in the form we believe we have experienced them. The sense of impotence before genocidal terror, man-made environmental disasters, and the progressive downfall of the Anthropocene emerges in the form of the numbness that follows the experience of non-existence. Extinction, therefore, becomes the only possibility for the translators to render the sense of *nisti* in the broader framework of the gap between human experience and the poet's personal experience of non-experience. The fear Jalali expresses in the poem (whose English rendition is one of the most beautiful pieces I have ever had the pleasure to read) is magisterially converted by the two translators into a chance for transformation—one that emerges from the vacuum generated by the desire of dying in a different *shape*:

i wish to die
not for my heart
        to stop beating

or my body to turn cold, level
              with the earth

i wish to die
    not to be severed from the world's echoes

      or the glimmer of sunlight
        or the sight of
           the moon and the stars

i wish to die a novel death

like the fading of water
      the sprouting of seeds

the sun's dissolution
    the sky's
        surrender to clouds

    i wish to stop existing &
        appear
      in another universe

one i have not named
    or tasted like

like the realm of dreams where
>   all is familiar

except the fear of extinction

>   & desperation

>   >   & solitude

Desiring Non-existence, or Lacking the Lack

Jalali's desire not to exist is radically different from the incessant dance with death that we find in Forugh Farrokhzad's poetry and life experiences, which include constant celebrations of the aesthetic value of the end of things as well as repeated suicide attempts (Ingenito 2023).[2] His desire is also distinct from the annihilation of selfhood (*fanā*) sought by medieval mystics through spiritual training and ascetic practices—an impulse that re-emerged in the 20th century with the neo-mystical pan-Eurasian voice of a poet like Sohrab Sepehri or in some of Bijan Elahi's most sibylline compositions (Sepehri 2021; Elahi, 2019). If we accept the Lacanian perspective that human desire is primarily driven by the perceived experience of existential lack, post-romantic

---

[2] For a critical edition of Forugh Farrokhzad's collected poems, along with an Italian translation, see Farrokhzad 2023.

existentialist poets like Forugh Farrokhzad cultivated the biographical and artistic possibilities of death as a radical solution to the realization that no experience, however intensely fulfilling, will ever fill their inner void.[3] For the mystic, non-existence is not a psychologically impairing void which ought to be feared. On the contrary, it constitutes a reflection of the highest form of being in the world—an escape from the illusion of individual subjectivity into divine unity (Ingenito, 2024a). Existential lack is thus embraced with the realization that being's fractures are completely filled by Being's presence.

In contrast, Jalali's desire for non-existence is neither the existentialist's tragic confrontation with lack nor the mystic's ecstatic realization that nothing truly exists in the face of the Divine presence. His poetry does not stage the drama of a self struggling against its own annihilation, nor does it seek transcendence through negation. Instead, it enacts a flattening of subjectivity, where even the experience of lack becomes muted, irrelevant, or imperceptible. What he experiences is the lack of a lack, or the ultimate silence of poetry.

If Farrokhzad's dance with death remains an artistic affirmation of life—an attempt to aestheticize

---

[3] For preliminary approaches to the application of Lacanian psychoanalysis to the study of Sufi mysticism and medieval Persian literature, see Sells and Webb, 1995; Tourage 2007; Kashani 2024.

annihilation—and if Sepehri's mysticism seeks to erase selfhood in order to witness the oneness of all existing things, Jalali's work can exist only after both possibilities have collapsed. His poetry does not desire death as an event, nor non-being as a goal, but rather registers the condition of already having disappeared. His verses unfold in a space of numb survival, where language no longer marks the struggle between being and non-being but merely records the trace of an already-erased self.

Jalali's non-existence, then, is not a metaphysical quest, an aesthetic obsession, or an existential rebellion—it is the simple recognition that there is nothing left to erase, nothing left to merge with, and no dramatic lack to fill. His is a poetics of the already-absent, a language that does not move toward the threshold of death or the limit of experience, but instead lingers in a world where the subject has faded into the static silence of the non-speakable.

What Jalali expresses in his poetry is a form of non-desire. In fact, whenever erotic desire makes its appearance, Jalali portrays it as an intangible possibility that is neither sensual nor intellectual. The few anonymous women he describes as potential objects of desire amount to the desireless contemplation of the incessant deferral of signifiers from their referents. Contrary to the physical presence of death-driven and-pleasure-principle-driven manhood in Forugh

Farrokhzad's poetry ("my man stands like Death," Farrokhzad, 2023, p. 552), objects of desire in Jalali's unerotic lines are not even a "thing" (let alone the Lacanian "Thing"), but rather words that meet no objects. Lack of experience—the impossibility of experiencing experience—is caught up in the movement of words that reach for meanings which do not exist. This is the core of the numbness that pervades Jalali's life and works. This is the stillness that precedes *jouissance* and prevents the death drive from experiencing the painful pleasure of the world as a compulsive activity:

in all eyes
i searched for you
in every body
i traced you

now i greet you
in all eyes
and see you
in all bodies

Undesiring the Fetish in the Face of the Non-Being

Things and words ask to be recognized as identical entities, yet the poet perceives the gap that separates them and gets lost in their constant lack of correspondence. While Jalali's object of desire is both non-erotic and non-mystical, it places itself between the erotic and the mystical (that is, between literary modernity and classical poetry) and gestures towards both while simultaneously denying them. The evanescence of the *You* prevents the *I* from existing by means of experience. Experience, therefore, becomes a linguistic afterthought—a possibility that never took place, or one among the "forgotten futures" that, according to Mark Fisher, characterize capitalist hyper-realism and the spectacle of genocidal death that has no spectators but its own self-replication (Fisher, 2009).

I have argued elsewhere that in important mystical trends of medieval Persian poetry, the object of desire is represented as a fetishized presence that means nothing unless read as a sign pointing towards celestial beauty and an attestation to the unfathomable creative powers of the divine (Ingenito, 2020, pp. 151–177; Ingenito, 2024b). Iranian literary modernity dissolved in a variety of ways the idea of the beloved as a fetish that signifies metaphysical beauty. Sadeq Hedayat's short story, "The Doll Behind the Curtain" (*'Arusak-e posht-e parde*), for instance, tells the story of a young Iranian student who moves to France and, having experienced social and psychological alienation, falls in love with a mannequin (Hedayat, 2011). The tragic event surrounding his libidinal attachment to an inorganic object of desire exemplifies the loss of projected metaphysical meaning that had sustained Persian literary eroticism for centuries, both in its mystical and obscene manifestations (Ingenito 2020). Jalali's representation of the object of visual contemplation goes one step further: it erases both the meaning of the object as an object and the object itself:

again i place
your green eyes
on your face

i who had
thieved them
for never ending
moments

The object is here a non-object that stands beyond the difference between the organic and the inorganic, removed from reality and preserved in an infra-imaginal or supra-imaginal space. Ultimately, this non-object is a non-existing object that mirrors the *I*'s will not to exist. The romance the poet might have longed for does not take place in time but rather within the contingency of the non-existent—of *non-Being*. When faced with a lack of experience, the *I*-lover melancholically holds onto the body parts of the object of desire, suspending them in a state of imagination-less longing. The beloved's body parts, their eyes, are therefore returned to their non-existent origin, undisturbed. The promise of "never ending / moments" represents the self-defeating fulfillment of a desire that never emerged from the poet's body.

Enjambment and the End of Things, Where Poetry Begins

The apparent randomness of Jalali's line breaks and the unpredictable enjambments they generate reveals that the truth of this poetry—and, as a consequence, the value of its experience—is shaped by the micro-silences that follow each broken and metrically obtuse line. With the *un*-rhythm of their shattered breath, Jalali's lines fully realize what Giorgio Agamben once described as the only criterion that defines poetry: the *possibility* of enjambment (Agamben, 1999). According to his theoretical stance, a line *is* poetry when its syntactical structure *may* carry over to the next line, thus potentially producing an enjambment. Agamben argues that, by this logic, the last line of a poem is not poetry, for the end of a syntactical string, however ungrammatical, terminates with the end of the final line. There is no carryover, no further possibility of saying anything beyond the final word of the final line. It is in that *non-poetry*—beyond what follows the last line of a poem—that Jalali's experience of poetry begins:

poetry begins
where all things
end

At this end of the end—where things end and poetry begins, where every line is a final line—the boundaries between reality and the artificial body of language become blurred. The touch of the real overshadows the power of imagination in a loop where not even mental idealizations can overshadow the relentless presence of non-existence:

reality always shatters
        my dreams
and every time
i see
reality is better
than my dreams

It turns out that for Jalali reality is more ideal than the dream, because it forecloses experience in a way that subverts the excess of the same mental constructions described by Fernando Pessoa when forcing his "heteronym," Alvaro de Campos, to confront the dissonance between the dullness of experience and the heights of delusional projections:

Today I'm bewildered, like a man who wondered and discovered and forgot.
Today I'm torn between the loyalty I owe
To the outward reality of the Tobacco Shop across the street
And to the inward reality of my feeling that everything's a dream (Pessoa, 1998)

The alienating numbness of mental experiences that cannot redeem reality's non-existence finds its solution in the necessity of transforming selfhood into something completely *other*—by forcing the self into an absolute alterity, a non-human thing that happens beyond the boundaries of human experience. This is the space where poetry reveals the absolute alterity of language itself—pointing at its truth without ever explaining it:

i want to crawl
into the skins of animals
& see the world

with their eyes

perhaps i'll find meaning
vast as my despair

Queering Poetry's Numbness: Displacement and Trans-formation

The despair of becoming *other* than oneself coincides with the effort of transitioning as a means to overcome existential alienation. It is with the intensity of such transitions that meaning can finally happen. And this is the space where Jalali's intrinsic queerness can be brought to the fore, especially through the lens of the negative paradigms of recent queer critical theory. By intersecting their minimalist and almost aesthetically restrained approach to translation with the confusing exuberance of a style that they ascribe to E.E. Cummings's linguistic and typographic experimentalism, Fani and Talukder pay homage to Jalali's quest for a de-alienating self-othering. Thanks to their choices (including the texts that they selected for this anthology, as well as the title of the book), readers are offered the opportunity to witness the poet's absolute solitude in a state of numbness which, by accepting itself for what it is, defeats alienation and calls for a constant act of transformation.

Jalali's seemingly non-committed poetry embodies the queer possibility of opting out as an act of silent resistance—a resistance revolving around transformation, transition, and displacement. Opposed to the privileged but infuriatingly blinding experience of expats and gentrifiers, the experience of migrants and refugees teaches us that all decentering and displacement comes with a numbing pain—the pain of not belonging, of not fitting anywhere, of feeling diminished rather than enriched by a transition to a different space. The pain of never feeling wholly integrated, or whole tout court. It is also the experience of queer people who, struggling with the very idea of integration itself, prefer to experience decentering as their own means of centering (Ruti, 2017). In their case—and especially in the case of refugees and trans people—the impossibility of living one's own (native or desired) language is a larger symptom of a fracture that affects language itself.

Jalali teaches us that poetry, given its sensitive vantage point on both the powerful dimensions and the shortfalls of language, is the textual locus where this fracture manifests itself in its full decentering force. Translating poetry makes us present to this numbness and the pain of seeking refuge in something we cannot claim as ours. It queers us—bringing us closer to the experience of trans individuals whose dignity is denied by the binary policies of the state and the silencing force of its normalizing Law. Poetic expression, within and beyond the boundaries of silence, is thus the only *act* whose numbing pain may ultimately offer subjects the chance to resist the process of silencing and turn silence into a force of meaningful transformation:

the mouth of silence
opened and shut once
i repeat what i heard
endlessly

Domenico A. Ingenito
Los Angeles,
January 30 – March 15, 2025

References

Ahmed, Amr Taher. *La "Révolution littéraire": Étude de l'influence de la poésie française sur la modernisation des formes poétiques persanes au début du XXe siècle*, Verlag der Österreichischen Akademie der Wissenschaften, ÖAW, 2012.

Agamben, Giorgio. "The End of the Poem." Translated by Daniel Heller-Roazen, in *The End of the Poem: Studies in Poetics*. Stanford University Press, 1999, pp. 109–115.

Berman, Antoine. *La Traduction et la lettre ou l'Auberge du lointain*, Éditions du Seuil, 1999.

Elahi, Bijan. *High Tide of the Eyes*. Translated by Rebecca Ruth Gould and Kayvan Tahmasebian, The Operating System, 2019.

Fani, Aria. "A Silent Conversation with Literary History: Re-theorizing Modernism in the Poetry of Bizhan Jalāli." *Iranian Studies*, vol. 50, no. 4, 2017, pp. 523–552.

Fani, Aria. "The Allure of Untranslatability: Shafiʻi-Kadkani and (Not) Translating Persian Poetry." *Iranian Studies*, vol. 54, nos. 1–2, 2020, pp. 95–125.

Fani, Aria. *Reading across Borders: Afghans, Iranians, and Literary Nationalism*, University of Texas Press, 2024.

Farrokhzad, Forugh. *Io parlo dai confini della notte. Tutte le poesie*. Edited and translated by Domenico Ingenito, Bompiani, 2023.

Fisher, Mark. *Capitalist Realism: Is There No Alternative?* Zero Books, 2009.

Hartley, Julia. *Iran and French Orientalism: Persia in the Literary Culture of Nineteenth-Century France*, I.B. Tauris, 2024.

Hedayat, Sadeq. "The Doll Behind the Curtain." Translated by Homa Katouzian, in *Three Drops of Blood*, Mage Publishers, 2011, pp. 15–25.

Helder, Herberto. *Poesia toda*. Assírio & Alvim, 1990.

Ingenito, Domenico. "Tradurre Ḥāfeẓ: quattro divān attuali." *Oriente Moderno*, 89, 1, 2009, pp. 151–171.

Ingenito, Domenico. *Beholding Beauty: Sa'di of Shiraz and the Aesthetics of Desire in Medieval Persian Poetry*, Brill, 2020.

Ingenito, Domenico. "Ti unisco al fuoco: appunti per una biografia poetica." In Farrokhzad 2023, pp. 5–35.

Ingenito, Domenico. "Al-Ghazālī (d. 505/1111) on Visionary Experiences and the Internal and External Senses." In *Islamic Sensory History. Volume 2: 600–1500*, eds. Christian Lange and Adam Bursi, Brill, 2024a, pp. 364–381.

Ingenito, Domenico. "Saʿdī (d. 691/1292) on the Senses, the Body, and Imagination." In *Islamic Sensory History. Volume 2: 600–1500*, eds. Christian Lange and Adam Bursi, Brill, 2024b, pp. 476–498.

Ingenito, Domenico. "Nezāmi's Story of the Competition Between Painters and Painting as Visual Meta-Poetic Gestures on Mimesis: From Takhyil, Mohākāt, and Takhayyol to Analogy, Simulacrum, and Holography." *Journal of Persianate Studies*, forthcoming.

Ingenito, Domenico and Camilla Miglio. "Die Reise des Hāfez von Shiraz über Istanbul und Wien nach Weimar: Oder: 'Europa hatte nie eine reine Seele'." *Rivista dell'Istituto Italiano di Studi Germanici*, no. 2, 2013, pp. 247–265.

Javadi, Hasan. *Persian Literary Influence on English Literature*, Mazda, 2005.

Kashani, Ashkaan. "Emergence of the New: Negation and Transformation in the *Haft Paykar*." Conference paper, UCLA Yarshater Center & Iranian Studies Symposium and Workshop, *Nezāmi and the Iranian World*, organized and convened by Domenico Ingenito, Los Angeles, November 21-22, UCLA, Los Angeles.

Landau, Justine. *De rythme & de raison. Lecture croisée de deux traités de poétique persans du XIIIe siècle*, Presses de la Sorbonne Nouvelle / IFRI, 2013.

Losensky, Paul E. *Welcoming Fighānī: Imitation and Poetic Individuality in the Safavid-Mughal Ghazal*. Mazda Publishers, 1998.

Meschonnic, Henry. *Ethics and Politics of Translating*. Translated by Pier-Pascale Boulanger, John Benjamins B.V., 2011.

Miglio, Camilla. *Vita a fronte: saggio su Paul Celan*. Quodlibet, 2005.
Osimo, Bruno. *Manuale del traduttore. Guida pratica con glossario*. Milan, Hoepli, 2011.
Pessoa, Fernando. "The Tobacco Shop." Translated by Richard Zenith, in *Fernando Pessoa & Co.: Selected Poems*. Grove Press, 1998, pp. 235–245.
Ruti, Mari. *The Ethics of Opting Out: Queer Theory's Defiant Subject*. Columbia University Press, 2017.
Sells, Michael and James Webb. "Lacan and Bion: Psychoanalysis and the Mystical Language of Unsaying." *Theory and Psychology* 5, no. 2, 1995, pp. 195–215.
Sepehri, Sohrab. *The Eight Books: A Complete English Translation*, trans. Pouneh Shabani-Jadidi and Prashant Keshavmurthy, Brill, 2021.
Sonboldel, Farshad. *The Rebellion of Forms in Modern Persian Poetry: Politics of Poetic Experimentation*, Bloomsbury, 2024.
Tourage, Mahdi. *Rūmī and the Hermeneutics of Eroticism*, Brill, 2007.
Venuti, Lawrence. *The Translator's Invisibility: A History of Translation*, 2nd ed., Routledge, 2008.

SHAPE OF EXTINCTION

Jalali at Cafe Shuka in Tehran (Photograph by Peyman Hooshmandzadeh)

i wish to die
not for my heart
        to stop beating

or my body to turn cold, level
            with the earth

i wish to die
    not to be severed from the world's echoes

        or the glimmer of sunlight
          or the sight of
            the moon and the stars

i wish to die a novel death

like the fading of water
      the sprouting of seeds

the sun's dissolution
    the sky's
        surrender to clouds

    i wish to stop existing &
        appear
      in another universe

می‌خواهم بمیرم
نه اینکه قلبم از کار بایستد
و تنم سرد شود
و با خاک یکسان شوم
می‌خواهم بمیرم
نه اینکه هیچ صدایی به گوشم نرسد
و هیچ خورشیدی بر من نتابد
و از دیدن ماه و ستارگان
کور باشم
می‌خواهم به مرگی کاملا غیر عادی بمیرم
مرگی شبیه بخار شدن آب
روئیدنِ دانه
غروبِ خورشید
ابری شدن آسمان
می‌خواهم نیست شوم
تا در دنیای دیگری ظاهر شوم

one i have not named
      or tasted

like the realm of dreams where
all is familiar

except the fear of extinction

          & desperation

                  & solitude

دنیایی که هنوز آن را ننامیده‌ام
دنیایی که مزهٔ آن را کاملاً نچشیده‌ام
دنیایی شبیه عالم خیال

که در آن همه چیز عادی باشد
جز وحشت از نیستی
جز درماندگی
جز تنهایی

I want a woman
like a tree—
green leaves dancing
in the wind,

embrace open like branches,
laugh stirred by the depths
of earth spread over her fingertips

i want a woman like a tree, who flees

horizon to horizon
every sunrise
        and sunset

as she bemoans her captivity
        in the soil

زنی را می‌خواهم
که مانند درخت باشد
با برگ‌های سبزی که در باد می‌رقصند
آغوشش
چون شاخه‌های درخت باز باشد
و خنده‌اش
از تاریکی‌های زمین الهام گرفته
در سر انگشت‌هایش پراکنده شود
زنی می‌خواهم چون درخت
که هر طلوع و غروب
از افقی به افقی بگریزد
در حالی که از اسارت خود در خاک گریه می‌کند

in all eyes
i searched for you
in every body
i traced you

now i greet you
in all eyes
and see you
in all bodies

در همهٔ دیده‌ها
به جستجوی تو می‌آمدم
و در همهٔ تن‌ها
سراغ تو را می‌گرفتم
اکنون ترا در همهٔ دیده‌ها
سلام می‌گویم
و در همهٔ تن‌ها
ترا می‌یابم

past and future
  day and night
are vines
    that have grown
all over our arms
        and faces.

آینده و گذشته
و شب و روز
چون گیاهانی هستند
که بر دست و صورت ما
روییده‌اند

    if only poetry
        were a sharp blade

      i would plunge it into my chest
          with my own hands:

        my scream
       one with the razor's
            flash

کاش شعر
تیغ تیزی بود
و من با دست خود
آنرا در سینهٔ خود
جا می‌دادم
و فریاد من
و برق تیغ
یکی می‌شد

i bestow
       my sorrow
upon the blank page
for safekeeping

  the page will return it
          to you just as it was
fresh
    and heart-searing

غمِ خویش را
به صفحهٔ کاغذ
می‌سپرم
و کاغذ امانت‌دار
خوبی است
آن را همچنان
تازه و جانسوز
تحویل شما
خواهد داد

i wished to die in your voice
or drift with your voice

        or sit soundless within

your voice went by
like the wind, and I am still

        clutching at the hem of darkness.

آرزویم مُردن در صدای تو بود
یا رفتن با صدایت
یا خاموش شدن در صدایت
صدای تو چون باد گذشت
و من به دامنِ تاریکی
آویخته‌ام

how strange!
my poems are all i can offer
      to the world

the same poems
gifted to me
      by the world

عجیب است
تنها چیزی که می‌توانم
به جهان تقدیم کنم
شعرهایم است
که جهان به من
داده است

i fear some day
i'll suffocate under
a pile of my poems

fortunately
i have a long nose
       for breathing

می‌ترسم زیر بار دست نوشته
شعرهایم
خفه شوم
ولی خوشبختانه دماغ درازی
دارم
برای نفس کشیدن

poetry plunges
like a meteorite, wounds

    my shoulder
          & hands

poetry lands
like an earthquake
    and fate's prisons

quiver
all at once

شعر فرو می‌افتد
مثل یکی از سنگ‌های آسمانی
و گاه شانه‌های من
و گاه دست‌هایم را
زخمی می‌کند
شعر فرود می‌آید
چون زلزله‌ای
و تمام پنجره‌های تقدیر
با هم می‌لرزند

how astonished the eyes
of these white walls
that bear no imprint
of memory

where
i see no mark
of despair

چه نگاه خیره‌ای
دارند
این دیوارهای سفید
زیرا نقشی از خاطره
بر آن‌ها نیست
و خطّی از اندوه
بر آن‌ها نمی‌بینم

Ah how poetry carries me
like a boat
on infinite waters!

آه که چگونه شعر
مرا می‌برد
چون قایقی
بر آب‌های بی‌کرانه‌ای

reality always shatters
            my dreams
and every time
i see
reality is better
than my dreams

واقعیّت هر بار
رویاهای مرا در هم
می‌شکند
و هر بار می‌بینم
که واقعیت بهتر از
رویای من است

again i place
your green eyes
on your face

i who had
thieved them
for never ending
moments

دوباره چشمان سبزت را
در صورتت می‌گذارم
من که آن‌ها را برای
لحظه‌های بی‌پایان
دزدیده بودم

some of my verses
bind to fire
some to earth
some to wind & water

and as they burn
perish into soil
drown or fly
i watch

بعضی از شعرهایم
به آتش می‌پیوندند
بعضی به خاک
بعضی به آب و باد
و من سوختن یا خاک شدن
غرق شدن یا پرواز کردن آن‌ها را
تماشا می‌کنم

a way to exist:
inside words
like fish
dwelling in water

نوعی زیستن است
زیستن در کلمات
مثل ماهیان
که در آب
زندگی می‌کنند

despair
has halved the world:

one half is me
the other
          the world

ناامیدی جهان را
به دو نیم کرده است
نیمی من شده‌ام
و نیمی جهان

my hand
is not my own
nor my face
or voice

my poems
are a far cry

نه دستم مال من است
نه صورتم و نه صدایم
چه رسد به شعرهایم

poetry begins
where all things
end

شعر از آنجا شروع
می‌شود
که همه چیز تمام
می‌شود

poetry has washed
everything (your footprints,

your smile on the wall)

& carried my voice
        to the precipice

                of words

همه را شعر شُسته است
جای پای تو را
و لبخند تو را بر دیوار
و صدای مرا نیز همراه خود
بُرده است
تا پرتگاه کلمات

i will never recite
a poem more beautiful
than a tree

if only they hadn't chopped it
& turned it to paper

من شعری از درخت
زیباتر
نخواهم گفت
کاش درخت را
نبریده بودند
و کاغذی از درخت
نساخته بودند

the poet in this world
is an orphan:

of a world past

and a world
        yet to come

شاعر در این جهان
یتیم است
و به جهانی تعلّق دارد
که گذشته است
و به جهانی که هنوز
نیامده است

solitude
> death

and between them
a step:

a thing named poetry

چیزی به نام تنهایی
چیزی به نام مرگ
و این وسط یک گامی
چیزی به نام شعر

again it is
the boulder of thought
& the sea of imagination

& the winds of eternity
& the flames of fire

that set everything
but poetry
        aflame

باز هم صخرهٔ فکر است
و دریای خیال
و بادهای دائم
و شعله‌های آتش
که همه چیز را جز شعر
می‌سوزانند

O Lord
when they take the world
from you
you also will turn to
nothing

خداوندا
آنگاه که جهان را
از تو بگیرند
تو نیز
هیچ می‌شوی

for me
the world has become
a cracked jug
and God
—its wholesome wine—
has seeped
into the black soil

جهان برای من
چون کوزه شکسته‌ای
شده است
و خداوند
که شراب گوارای کوزه بود
در خاک تیره
فرو رفته است

my heart is a gate
behind which ephemeral love
pauses a moment

& once the gate opens
sets out
for eternity

دل من
چون دروازه‌ایست
که عشق‌های زودگذر
لحظه‌ای پشت آن توقف
می‌کند
و آنگاه که دروازه گشوده شد
به سوی ابدیّت
رهسپار می‌شوند

poetry is a fire:
it sets the world
ablaze but
makes it luminous

شعر
چون آتش است
که جهان را
می‌سوزاند
ولی آن را روشن
می‌کند

i have something
to say i have yet
to write
for it is whiter
than paper

حرفی دارم
که تا کنون
آن را ننوشته‌ام
زیرا سفیدتر از کاغذهاست

i want to crawl
into the skins of animals
& see the world
with their eyes

perhaps i'll find meaning
vast as my despair

می‌خواهم در پوست حیوانات
بخزم
و دنیا را از چشم آن‌ها
بنگرم
شاید معنایی را بیابم
به وسعت اندوه خود

the day i die
return to the sea
what i've held of it as keepsake
return to the sky
what's left of it in my heart

the humming of the forest
            the noise of the
waterfalls

       return them to the
forest
                    and
waterfalls

and if any stars
should remain in my hands
send them back to the sky

then return
my body to the earth
my heart
to dark and silence

آن روز که مُردم
آنچه را که یادگار دریاست
به دریا بازدهید
و آنچه را که از آسمان
در دل من مانده است
به آسمان بازگردانید
زمزمه‌ی جنگل
و صدای آبشارها را
به جنگل و آبشارها برگردانید
و اگر ستاره‌ای در دست‌های من مانده است
آن را به آسمان بازفرستید
و آنگاه تنِ من را به زمین باز دهید
و قلب من را به سکوت و تاریکی بسپارید

the sound of children crying
and the splendor of the sun
everywhere
are the same

صدای گریه کودکان
و درخشیدنِ
خورشید
در همه جا
یکسان است

how splendid
that a mortal heart would
hold an eternal love

چه خوب است
دلی باشد میرا
و در آن
عشقی باشد
جاودانه

when reality
is so unspeakable

one must resort to silence
                          or to verse

وقتی واقعیت ناگفتنی است
یا باید سکوت کرد
یا باید شعر گفت

if you
were here
the world would be a different color
your breath would mix
with the winds' forever movement

your gaze
would turn the sky
deeper, bluer

اگر تو
این جا بودی
جهان رنگِ دیگری داشت
نفَسِ تو
با حرکتِ بی‌پایانِ بادها
می‌آمیخت
از نگاهِ تو
آسمان عمیق‌تر و آبی‌تر می‌شد

the silence of words
cages me
within myself

O people
you hear my cries,
fathom these words
bursting with
my silence

the day you come to me
it will be too late
i will have turned
another way

you will sift in vain
through the words' silence
searching for my voice

سکوتِ کلمات
مرا در خود گرفته‌اند
ای مردمان
صدای مرا می‌شنوید
که به سوی شما می‌آید
کلمات را می‌شناسید
که انباشته از سکوتِ
من هستند
ولی دیرگاه خواهند بود
آن روزی که به سراغ من می‌آیید
من رو به سوی دیگر
خواهم داشت
و شما بیهوده
در سکوتِ کلمات
صدای مرا جستجو خواهید
کرد

i cleanse myself
in the sound
of waves

the sea has roared
a thousand years

and i am a pebble
resting on the seabed

در صدای موج‌ها
شستشو می‌کنم
و گوئیا هزاران هزار سال است
که دریا می‌خروشد
و من چون سنگی
در کفِ آن آرمیده‌ام

how much of a poet
must one be

to see a flower
to recite a flower

چقدر باید شاعر بود
تا گُلی را بتوان دید
تا گُلی را بتوان گفت

my beloved is poetry–

each time a verse is written,
an embrace

معشوق من شعر است
و هر شعر وقتی نوشته می‌شود
یک وصال است

my black cat
is a sliver
of the night

گربهٔ سیاه من
یک تکه از
شب است

in my mind words clamor
like stray children, wandering
in search of their own
poems

کلمات چون کودکان ولگرد
هیاهو می‌کنند
و در خیالِ من می‌گذرند
کلماتِ سرگردان
که به دنبالِ شعرِ خود
می‌گردند

whether i open
the notebook
or close it
poems fly
ceaselessly everywhere

دفتر را باز کنم
یا دفتر را ببندم
شعرها همیشه و همه جا
در پروازند

i wish that you were a goddess
you'd rest by my side
like the sea
one by one i'd catch
the fish of your breasts
then return them
to the waves

تو کاش الهه‌ای بودی
و در کنار من می‌آرمیدی
چون دریا
و من ماهیان سینه‌ات را
یکایک شکار می‌کردم
و سپس به امواج دریا
باز پس می‌دادم

at the world's feet:
fallen leaves of
earth's
autumn

کلمات در پای جهان
فرو می‌ریزند
چون برگ‌های خزانی
جهان

the page is like a river
i pour in
my sorrow
so that it gets lost
in the sea

so that i
forget it

صفحهٔ کاغذ چون رودی است
و من غم خود را به او
می‌سپارم
تا آن را در دریا گم کند
و آن را فراموش کنم

poetry is free of where
it is and why it is
and where it goes

شعر فارغ است
از اینکه کجاست
و چرا هست
و کجا می‌رود

madness from these parts
passes. i know it
in an instant:
he recites a poem
cryptic, nonsensical

دیوانگی از این طرف‌ها
می‌گذرد
او را ندیده می‌شناسم
زیرا شعری می‌خواند
نامفهوم

my night's end
is always blank
i end it
with a page
in my hand

پایان شبِ من
همواره سفید است
زیرا با کاغذی در دست
آن را به پایان
می‌رسانم

i have no secrets
i just retell
the secret of the blank page

من رازی ندارم
فقط راز کاغذ سفید را
باز می‌گویم

the mouth of silence
opened and shut once
i repeat what i heard
endlessly

دهان سکوت
یک‌بار باز و بسته شد
و آنچه را که شنیدم
همواره تکرار
می‌کنم

i scattered myself
in four corners of the world
but the wind put me back together
and poetry took me with itself

من خودْ را پراکنده کردم
در چهار گوشهٔ جهان
ولی باد مرا به هم پیوست
و شعر مرا همراه خود برد

i brought death,
a companion

with it
i spent my life
and i will take it
with me

مرگ را همراه خود
آورده‌ام
با او زندگی کرده‌ام
و او را همراه خود
خواهم برد

i remove language
from the path,
place it aside

to recite
a poem without
a tongue

زبان را از راه
برمی‌دارم
زبان را کنار
می‌گذارم
تا شعری گفته باشم
بی‌زبان

i have arrived at
my poetry's root:
                         death

i bury my verse
      at its feet

به حرف اصلی شعرم
رسیده‌ام
یعنی به مرگ
و شعرم را در پای آن
به خاک می‌سپارم

the ailing cat
who licks her hand
thinks of the entire universe

and what all the other cats
have told her

گربهٔ ناخوش
که دستش را می‌لیسد
گوئیا به همه کیهان
فکر می‌کند
و آنچه که همه گربه‌ها
به او گفته‌اند

on the tree of the world
the mythical
        bird of words
                              sits
& in her wide-eyed gaze
        in her cry

i see the world
                brighter

بر درختِ جهان
مرغ افسانهٔ کلام
نشسته است
و در نگاهش و در فریادش
جهان را روشن‌تر
می‌بینم

when the world
tells its story
it is of love
and when i tell it:
despair

جهان به روایت خودش
عشق است
و به روایت من
اندوه

i've died
spread over
some unspoken
poems

مُرده‌ام
و روی چند شعرِ ناگفته
خوابیده

a train
moves inside me
sometimes i go after it
and sometimes
i clamber atop

this train
is poetry

قطاری در من
حرکت می‌کند
گاهی دنبالش می‌روم
و گاهی سوارش هستم
این قطار شعر
است

In Quiet Revolt: The Poetic Legacy of Bijan Jalali
Aria Fani

"Poetry, especially yours, is like butterfly hunting—even when there are no butterflies to catch," remarked Baha al-Din Khorramshahi (b. 1945), the renowned literary critic and translator, in a conversation with Bijan Jalali (2004, p. 115). Another critic, Parviz Mohajer (d. 1976), likened Jalali's poetry to cotton candy and popcorn (Abedi, 2000; 208). The former was intended as a compliment, and the latter as a critique. Simin Behbahani (d. 2014), the celebrated lyric poet, described Jalali as a "nightingale whose singing is guided by innate intuition" (2000), perhaps without intending to offer either praise or critique. The frequent use of metaphors for a subject often reveals its resistance to being neatly classified. This is certainly the case with Bijan Jalali.

Jalali's standing in the modern poetry canon has been both unsettled and evolving. His work first appeared in the early 1960s and 1970s, but it wasn't until the 2000s that his poetry gained wider readership and critical acclaim. Jalali's poetics align more closely with the work of high modernists like Ahmad Shamlu (d. 2000) than with classically oriented poets like Behbahani. Yet, while Jalali was overlooked by the likes of Shamlu, he was more warmly received by conservative voices like Behbahani and Khorramshahi. Private and reserved,

Jalali did not shape or participate in consequential discussions about poetic modernism during the 1980s, a time when experimental avant-garde poetry was gaining prominence in the pages of such journals as *Adineh*, *Takapu*, *Gardun*, and *Donya-yi Sokhan* (Sonboldel, 2024). Jalali's poetics, however, were already advancing in that direction with remarkable foresight. How, then, can we begin to understand Bijan Jalali today?

Let's start here: Jalali is a modern poet. To be modern is to participate in transforming a centuries-old poetic tradition with its established conventions, genres, and aesthetic norms. Poetic modernism, like modernity itself, doesn't have a single path but many. Ahmad Karimi-Hakkak's now-classic *Recasting Persian Poetry* outlined "scenarios of poetic modernism" that gradually became mainstream. This particular lineage of modernism, with its roots in Iran's Constitutional Revolution (1906–1911), reached its pinnacle in the work of Nima Yushij (born Ali Esfandiyari, d. 1960). *The Rebellion of Forms in Modern Persian Poetry* by Farshad Sonboldel has recently addressed what *Recasting Persian Poetry* briefly acknowledged, presenting a broader and more inclusive perspective on overlooked poetic modernisms in Iran. In fact, reading Sonboldel's work inspired Adeeba and me to finally find a home for Jalali's work in English.

The poems in your hands are the result of fifteen years of friendship and collaboration. I met Adeeba during a summer workshop for teachers of Persian, Arabic, and Hindi/Urdu at NYU in 2010. Adeeba's passion for Urdu poetry naturally extended to a deep respect for the Persian poetic tradition. I had also, perhaps more naively, become enthusiastic about literary translation, writing a column titled "Persian Poetry Today" for a bilingual cultural magazine called *Peyk*. Throughout this time, Adeeba and I refined two dozen drafts, working to render Jalali's voice in an engaging and dynamic English style. Along the way, the bylines on our cover letters to literary publishers changed, reflecting our own journeys. Adeeba earned an MFA in poetry from the University of Michigan and published two acclaimed poetry collections: *What Is Not Beautiful* (2018) and *Shahr-e-jaanaan: The City of the Beloved* (2020). She has become a stunning singer of ghazal poetry, deeply influenced by the orality of Urdu's rich poetic tradition.

I too accomplished a couple of things, working as an assistant professor at the University of Washington in 2019, and publishing my first book, *Reading across Borders: Afghans, Iranians, and Literary Nationalism* (2024). Adeeba and I are deeply grateful that these poems have finally found their way into the world. In some ways, we're glad the process took as long as it did. Jalali's meditative, unpretentious poetry deserves to linger in your thoughts for a while! Through different thematic vignettes, this essay will explore key facets of Jalali's poetry, its reception, and its qualities in Persian and in translation. What will unfold here is a complete portrait of a poet whose reclusive and private nature initially kept him in the shadow of more charismatic, outspoken poets like Shamlu, only for him to eventually embrace the role of a public-facing poet.

Poetics of Free Verse

Jalali's chosen form is free verse. His poems do not adhere to the conventional meters of both classical and Nimaic prosodic structures, the former considered to be the hallmark of Persian poetry. Classical prosody is based on a structure of two-hemistich lines arranged in columns, with a monorhyme at the end of each line and a consistent meter repeated throughout. Nima reconfigures this structure as we will later see. In the only English-language article on Jalali's poetry prior to my 2017 essay in *Iranian Studies*, Masʿud Zavarzadeh highlights that Jalali was one of the few poets — if not the only in his generation— who avoided experimenting with classical forms and prosodic structures, composing exclusively in free verse (1984).

In Persian, there are various models of free verse. Jalali's work leans more toward prose poetry or *sheʿr-e mansur*, unlike Shamlu's free verse, which, while non-prosodic and non-rhythmic, remains distinctly musical.

The question of terminology necessarily requires addressing the incommensurability that exists both among and within languages. The English term "free verse" is less an exact equivalent for Jalali's poetic form than an approximation. In both languages, free verse functions as a broad designation encompassing a wide range of innovations in metrical structures, diction, imagery, and other elements of poetic form. This account of free verse itself draws on French modernist poetry and its historiographical lineage. In Persian, the term "free verse," translated as *she'r-e azad*, remains an unsettled concept. While Nima Yushij was instrumental in breaking away from the prosodic patterns of classical poetry, his work still adheres to its own metrical structures, making the application of "free verse" somewhat inaccurate. Therefore, he warrants a category of his own: Nimaic poetry, or *she'r-e Nima'i*. Some of the younger generation's poetic output that emulated him may be described as Nimaic poetry, though not all fits this label.

While we might use "free verse" to describe the works of both Jalali and Shamlu, musicality remains central to the latter's poetics. All three poets, however, would fall under the broad and nebulous category of "modern poetry," or *she'r-e now*, whose origins, according to conventional wisdom, trace back to Nima's poetic innovations of the 1960s and 1970s. The terrain of poetic modernism, like Jalali's work and its reception, remains ever-shifting. Literary studies has begun to engage with poetic modernism within a more global framework, emphasizing cross-cultural exchanges and the shared yet uneven processes of modernization. By situating Jalali's poetry within both Persian and anglophone contexts, my hope is to foreground modernism not as a singular and linear cultural phenomenon, but rather a series of overlapping and plural modernisms experienced differently across time and space.

Poetry or Prose?

In Persian literary culture more broadly, poetry (*she'r*) has often been defined in opposition to prose (*nasr*). Many critics in the 1970s and 1980s frequently characterized Jalali's poetry as prose-like in order to dismiss it. In the 1992 edition of *Gold in Copper* (*Tala dar mes*), Baraheni takes a poem by Jalali, removes its line breaks, and questions what makes it poetry. Earlier in the 1960s, Jalali's work had been likened to cotton candy, devoid of any value or substance. Although one could interpret it differently than intended by the critic, cotton candy does have a way of sticking with you longer than expected!

Three decades later, prose poetry in Persian can no longer be dismissed as easily, having found recognition as a legitimate form. A closer look at Jalali's work, free from labels, reveals how it fits into modern trends in

Persian poetry. Jalali's verse shares many similarities with minimalism. His language is pared down; most of his poems consist of thirty words or fewer, and his longer poems rarely exceed sixty. Repetition is key—words like *yā* (or), *va* (and), and *gah* (at times) appear frequently, helping to mark shifts in thought and rhythm. These words also give his poems a musical quality. The way his poems appear on the page—brief, simple, and uncluttered—further signals their modern quality, distinguishing them from prose.

Jalali's poetics align more closely with the modernist Mohammad Moqaddam (d. 1996) who preceded him. According to Sonboldel, Moqaddam should be seen as the poet who pioneered free verse and introduced it to Persian-language readers. On the impact of Moqaddam's poetic legacy, Sonboldel writes,

> …Moqaddam's freestyle rhyme liberates the poem from a rigid structure, injecting a sense of rhythmic variety and breaking the monotony of the poetic rhythm. It was the use of freestyle rhyme that, in time, altered the entire narrative system of Persian poetry and gave distinctive voices to different elements within the poem (2024; 131-132)

In the case of both Moqaddam and Jalali, critics uncritically attribute their modern poetics to their consumption of Western poetry in translation. One might ask, however, are classically oriented poets immune to the influences carried by translation? In Iranian literary historiography, translation has become a byword for change or even rupture. We should move beyond symbolic treatments of translation and recognize it as generating distinct and conflicting effects in the target language that require careful analysis. Passive assertions such as "Poet X was influenced by poetry Y in translation" obscure the complex variables of agency, mediation, and reception.

The most salient quality of Jalali's poetry is its simplicity: the absence of ornate language, complex vocabulary, and convoluted expressions. Poetic simplicity is far from effortless and plays a key role in Jalali's effort to create a distinctive voice that sets him apart from the dominant literary trends of his time. Jalali's figurative language may seem straightforward, especially in contrast to the intricate, often surreal, and allegorical style that dominated Persian poetry during this period. These traditional styles required readers to decode social and political references embedded within the text. Modern poets had the freedom to experiment with symbolism and metaphor, often creating works that demanded prior knowledge to fully understand their layered meanings. Jalali, however, steers away from these complexities, opting for a more accessible and transparent style. In 1992, Jalali described his commitment to simplicity in a way that underscores his rejection of highly conventionalized poetry:

> My poems are simple and easy to read; they come from everyday Persian. This simplicity shouldn't be seen as a unique quality. To me, poetry should be simple and direct. But since most modern poetry is hard to read, the simplicity of my poems may be their greatest strength. They flow naturally, born from a true urge, not a desire to create a literary artifact.

While many poets believed that the use of complex symbols and allegory was poetry's social duty. In the late 1990s and early 2000s, poetic circles began to more systematically translate philosophers Jacques Derrida, Roland Barthes, Jean François Lyotard, and Jean Baudrillard (Sonboldel, 2024). This theoretical turn in the poetry of *dah-ye haftad* (the 1370s) introduced more webs of referentiality into modern poetry. Jalali questions how easily readers can navigate layers of intertextuality. His work subtly critiques the notion that poetry must be complex to be relevant. However, this pursuit of clarity and directness has not always been well received. Ahmad Karimi-Hakkak, one of Jalali's first English translators speaks of the poet's "zealous desire" for clarity, noting that his poems can sometimes come across as "anticonventional in form and stark in meaning" (1994; 83). In an observation that carries a hint of value judgment, Karimi-Hakkak notes that his poems may risk veering too closely toward prose aphorisms or pseudo-philosophical musings.

Some of Jalali's first poems, published in his 1962 debut collection *Ruz'ha* (Days), validate this critique. Consider this poem: "My God / every night is a journey into eternity / every day / every moment of the day / is a journey into eternity." The poem presents its central idea—"the eternity of the present"—right from the start, and then repeats the concept in the following lines, offering no new insight or movement. In his later collections, particularly from the 1990s onwards, Jalali sought to better balance simplicity and depth of imagery.

Modern poetics

As earlier mentioned, Persian poetic modernism is inextricably tied to Nima Yushij, the "father of *she'r-e now*"—because poetry, like the nation-state, apparently needed a father figure to finally step into the modern age (Sonboldel offers a different genealogy, see "Dismantling the Poetic Father"). Nima's oeuvre by and large represents a strict adherence to (more so in earlier works) and a generative reconfiguration (in later works) of Perso-Arabic prosody. Levi Thompson's *Reorienting Modernism in Persian and Arabic Poetry* insists on taking seriously the question of meter (and metrical experimentation) in the making of modern poetic forms. Thompson characterizes Nima's poetic project as such,

> In consideration of Nīmā's incorporation of premodern formal and thematic elements into his New Poetry, I argue that he sublates the past into the present in his poems. Throughout, I compare Nīmā's process of sublation with the Pahlavi dynasty's fabrication of a national myth by reformulating the Iranian past in their attempt to institute modernity in Iran (2022; 21)

Unlike Nima, Jalali's verse sidesteps the millennial tradition of Perso-Arabic altogether. For instance, the way poetry appears on the page, its most basic materiality, for readers acquainted with classical Persian invokes this scheme:

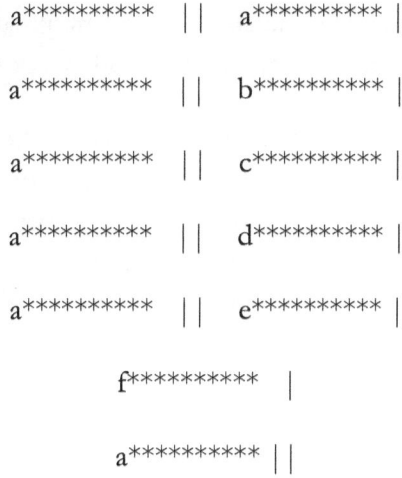

In reformulating classical prosodic structures, Nima tends to place his breaks where an idea ends, as opposed to a rhyme. On the other hand, the way Jalali's poems appear on the page signals not a reformulation of poetic pasts but the birth of a new tradition. He relies on enjambments—his tendency to run sentences across lines without pause—that seem quite arbitrary in his earlier works (or done with less intentionality). When asked to explain his use of enjambment, Jalali said he envisioned his poetry cascading across the page like rain. The visual and rhythmic layout of his poems plays a crucial role in their form.

Jalali's earlier poems were much longer, but he eventually settled on short poems. There is a minimalist quality to his work. And here I don't wish to imply that only the short can be minimalist. In an essay on poetic minimalism, Gerald Janecek writes:

> Minimalism makes use of quite humble linguistic materials, the verbal equivalent of found objects, and uses them in provocative ways. It forces us, through artifice, to pay attention to these humble materials and discover hidden riches within them (1992; 418).

Jalali not only finds aesthetic value in the simplest elements of language but also challenges the conventional meanings attached to everyday objects.

Words like *walls, trees, papers, words, poetry,* and *beloved* take on new, more intimate functions in his work, far removed from the overt political symbolism found in much contemporary poetry. Following the Iranian Revolution, activists assigned new meanings to ordinary objects—trees became watchtowers, newspapers carried revolutionary messages, and walls became canvases for protest. But Jalali avoids such political readings. For him, walls are simply "memories of bygone days" or the smile of a beloved friend:

poetry has washed
everything (your footprints,
your smile on the wall)
& carried my voice
       to the precipice
              of words

همه را شعر شسته است
جای پای تو را
و لبخند تو را بر دیوار
و صدای مرا نیز همراه خود برده است
تا پرتگاه کلمات

The poetic "I" is not just a grammatical entity; it speaks both publicly and privately, politically and philosophically. The modernism of the 1960s and 1970s measured poetry's value by its social relevance, with the assumption that a collective voice could achieve this. While not all modern poems insist on a more representational rhetoric, many Iranian literary critics did emphasize the collective voice, encouraging readers to interpret the "I" as "we." The implications of this approach for reading modern poetry remain largely unexplored.

Jalali's poetic speaker, however, does not represent the formulated collective. Jalali's subject is fragmented, individualistic, and does not reconcile to the collectivist fervor of his time. At a moment when the poetic "I" was often read as "we," the singular became an act of resistance—a deliberate flight from the collectivist mold. Seen through another lens, Jalali's poems, though not its subject, echo shared anxieties and ruminations, representing, in a way, a silent and politically unworked collective. His work does so through its meditation on extinction, on nonbeing.

Jalali's use of "man," the Persian first-person singular, becomes a gesture toward individual subjectivity. In Persian, pronouns are often superfluous, both grammatically and semantically. Yet Jalali's frequent use of "man" underscores his subjective universality. Indeed in most classical poems, the poet does not employ the first-person pronoun. By the 1980s and 1990s, critics began to view his poetic voice as part of a broader movement to define the modern poet's role. Kamyar Abedi notes, "The poetic 'I' only gains meaning when existence is placed at the center of its attention, pointing toward immortality ... time in the poems of Jalali reaches the threshold of nonexistence. Time is invisible in his poetry; it is timelessness" (2000; 41). Consider the following:

گاه می‌پندارم چون حافظ راه می‌روم
یا چون سعدی می‌نشینم
یا خیام‌وار جام را خالی می‌کنم
گاه همراه مسعود سعد در زندان
یا همراه فرخی در خیمه سلطان هستم
و در پایان خود را همچون خود
و همچون همیشه تنها می‌بینم

at times i imagine
i walk upon the path like Hafez
sit like Sa'di
empty my wine cup like Khayyam
share a prison cell
with Mas'ud-e-Sa'd
or stay with Farrokhi in the Sultan's tent
and in the end i see myself
as myself
always
in solitude

Jalali's poetic voice aligns itself with the tradition of canonical Persian poets, all of whom lived in premodernity. While these figures are celebrated for their verse, Jalali emphasizes ordinary actions that connect them as humans, transcending the act of writing poetry. Saʿdi is renowned for his extensive travels, while Hafez is known for rarely leaving his native Shiraz (admittedly, every Nowruz the present writer wishes he hadn't left Shiraz either). Yet Jalali imagines himself both "sitting" like Saʿdi and "walking" like Hafez. Khayyam is famously associated with a cup, a clear reference to the central role of wine in his *rubaʿiyat*. Farrukhi flourished as a panegyrist in the Ghaznavid court, while Masʿud-e Saʿd, another Ghaznavid poet, penned his renowned *habsiyāt* (prison poems) during his imprisonment. In a handful of lines, Jalali has brought these celebrated Persian poets down to earth, figures who had been incorporated — materially and intellectually— into the nation's pantheon in the Pahlavi era.

Jalali's poetic "I" in this poem does something noteworthy. Most modern poets invoked past poetic figures in order to break from (or forge a shared lineage in some cases) those poets who had been enshrined as national institutions. Jalali's portrayal of walking with Hafez contrasts with an irreverent and non-believing Hafez in Shamlu's work. Jalali also keeps company with both Masʿud-e Saʿd and Farrukhi, while Reza Baraheni (at least in the 1960s) elevates Masʿud as a champion of committed poetry and predictably dismisses Farrukhi as an elitist court poet. Jalali's poetic voice neither rejects nor explicitly endorses the literary pasts; instead, he exists in his cultural legacy, and yet in solitude. It is within this imagined solitude that he reflects on the very nature of poetry.

Reflections on Poetry

The twentieth century saw the emergence of a critical body of texts central to modern poetic practice, texts that define poetry and its evolving role in the world. This is particularly evident in the work of Nima, whose epistolary prose reflects on his poetry and explores the challenges of writing modern verse. While his poetological writings are as expansive as his poetic output, systematic studies in English addressing Nima's theories didn't emerge until the 1990s. The question of poetics is also a central theme in many modern poems, where poetry itself becomes aware of its status as verse, actively reflecting on its form and purpose. Few poets have written as extensively on poetry as Bijan Jalali. His collections *On Poetry* (1998) and *Encounters* (2001) are dedicated to such meditations, with numerous other poems on the subject scattered throughout his works. Yet, Jalali's metapoetic writings have remained largely overlooked in critical discussions.

Metapoetry refers to poems that explore poetry itself, and Jalali's works on this theme stand out for their depth. He doesn't just reflect on the act of writing; he personifies poetry, granting it agency. For Jalali, poetry is not merely an act of composition—it is intertwined with his very being: "my beloved is poetry– / each time a verse is written, / an embrace." Orientalist translators have long rendered *vesāl* and *vasl* as "union," but these terms may primarily be read as erotic, meaning "encounter" and "embrace." In Sufi poetry, they signify brief contact with the unseen, and not necessarily with God (see *Beholding Beauty*). Jalali uses the idea of vesal to describe his own pursuit—poetry. The union between poet and poetry is not a final, stable state for Jalali; rather, it is fragile, characterized by vulnerability and an ongoing struggle to define his relationship with the elusive "beloved" that is poetry itself. In his other poems, Jalali emphasizes the fleeting nature of this union, illustrating how he never truly owns his work and is constantly thwarted by the task of composing poetry.

نه دستم مال من است
نه صورتم و نه صدایم
چه رسد به شعرهایم

my hand
is not my own
nor my face
or voice

my poems
are a far cry

Jalali's speaker cannot claim ownership of his poems, for they constantly slip through his fingers. At times, he lives with his poetry, even taking it out for fresh air; at other times, it is poetry that lives in his place. He may use poetry to face death, yet at other moments, his poems emerge from death—or he even dies within them. He may try to tell us where poetry can be found, but in the end, he comes up empty-handed, waging war against poetry and once again encountering defeat.

به جنگ شعر رفتن
و یکبار دیگر تجربه شکست را
آزمودن

going to war against poetry
and once more
experiencing defeat

The syntax here is ambiguous: *beh jang-e she'r raftan* (going to war against poetry). Is the speaker marching to war for poetry's sake—fighting in defense of poetry, rather than against it? Given Jalali's other metapoetic works, in which he frames the act of composition as a battle (such as poetry as a "battlefield" or an "adversary"), I am inclined to interpret the speaker as going to war *against* poetry. The speaker engages in a struggle to subdue and conquer *she'r*, only to return nearly defeated. But the act of writing poetry entails more than just defeat; it signifies loss for a poet whose subject lives more fully than his words. In this instance, the poetic subject must sacrifice living itself to breathe life into an ode to its own beauty.

من شعری از درخت
زیباتر
نخواهم گفت
کاش درخت را
نبریده بودند
و کاغذی از درخت
نساخته بودند

i will never recite
a poem more beautiful
than a tree

if only they hadn't
chopped it and turned it to paper

Jalali's metapoetic works converse with one another in multiple ways. When considered as a cohesive poetic corpus, they also engage with popular assumptions and theories about poetry. As previously noted, modern poets have produced a diverse range of writings aimed at defining poetry. A critical examination of interviews, monographs, and manifestos from the twentieth century reveals a wide array of differing views and visions on the subject. While these works share a common goal—defining the essence of poetry—there are sharp contrasts in their approaches. Many committed poets argue that the essence of poetry lies in its social function. In response, a wave of anti-commitment poets sought to free poetry from this prescribed essence. Yet, in their attempt to detach poetry from its social function, they inadvertently sought to establish a new essence for it. In a tradition determined to redefine itself, the question of poetry's essence remains pivotal. I argue that Jalali's metapoetry abandons the modern search for an essence, instead wrestling with poetry as a free and elusive entity.

شعر فارغ است
از اینکه کجاست

و چرا هست
و کجا می رود

poetry is free of where
it is and why it is
and where it goes

The poetic speaker is always in pursuit of the poetic moment, yet finds himself immersed in the ordinariness of daily life. In other words, there is no trace of the divinely inspired moment in Persian literary culture—the prophet-like poet, the original creator, imagined as connected to a world beyond (existing alongside other ideas of poetic creation). In this regard, Jalali also appeared to be ahead of his time. The nature of the poet became a hotly debated topic in the 1990s, though his work was notably absent from these discussions (see, for instance, Fallah, 2001). In Jalali's work, readers encounter many sources of poetic inspiration, both divine and mundane, spontaneous and premeditated. These moments of creation coexist, never privileged or overshadowed by any singular, absolute origin. One vision places agency in the poet's hands, who is keenly aware of the limitations of language; another sees the poet as a passive recipient, helpless in the face of poetry's unpredictable mercy. Consider these two poems:

زبان را از راه
بر می‌دارم
زبان را کنار
می‌گذارم
تا شعری گفته باشم
بی‌زبان

i remove language
from the path,
place it aside

to recite
a poem without
a tongue

~~~

شعر فرو می‌افتد
مثل یکی از سنگ‌های آسمانی
و گاه شانه‌های من
و گاه دست‌هایم را
زخمی می‌کند
شعر فرود می‌آید
چون زلزله‌ای
و تمام پنجره‌های تقدیر
با هم می‌لرزند

poetry plunges
like a meteorite, wounds

    my shoulder
        & hands

poetry lands
like an earthquake
    and fate's prisons

quiver
all at once

The first poem explores poetry as an act of removing, setting aside, or transcending language itself. Jalali's play on both meanings of "zaban" —tongue (the physical organ) *and* language (the medium)— is key here. His poem signals a desire to retreat from verbal articulation, highlighting the limits of spoken language in capturing deeper truths. its insufficiency for the expression of universal emotions or truths. But what would retreat from language look like? Jalali, and many in his cohort, would argue that Persian poetry had become too conventionalized in the course of its historical development and that those conventions prevent poets from finding a more intuitive form of expression. This too is a rhetorical posture, a distancing tactic that sets Jalali apart from Persian poets that had come before him.

The second poem presents poetry as a dynamic and violent force—a meteorite, an earthquake. It collides with the poet, leaving physical and emotional marks. In both poems, poetry exists beyond the boundaries of verbal language, in silence or in a state of ineffable being. A true poet is one who can get out of the way. And getting out of the way —with the goal of writing a poem without a tongue/language— comes with a great deal of vulnerability: the poet, physically wounded and verbally silent, nonetheless searching to articulate shared human experiences beyond language (yet through its medium). Metapoetry became more relevant in the 1990s, particularly among "language poets" such as Baraheni and Shams Aqajani who have composed well-received poems in this subgenre. Baraheni's own students went on to meditate on the idea of writing about writing, *neveshtan-e neveshtan* in their parlance. But none have looked at Jalali's experiments with metapoetry. Jalali's metapoetic works —which are many— have yet to be critically examined. We hope the publication of this book will bring more attention to his poetry.

Writing for Translation?

The discussion of Jalali's poetry in English would be incomplete without a critical consideration of the challenges of translation—an issue often relegated to a marginal note in literary analyses. In October 1992, a group of poets, translators, and literary enthusiasts convened to discuss Jalali's body of work. Among the attendees were Ahmad Reza Ahmadi and Shams Langarudi, along with others. The group unanimously agreed that Jalali's poetry is notably easier to translate compared to other modern Persian works. Omran Salahi, one participant, remarked that "Jalali's poetry is not adorned with poetic craft, a quality that contributes to its translatability." The group further noted that poetic form—rooted in systematic meter in classical Persian poetry—poses one of the greatest challenges in translation.

As previously discussed, Jalali's poetic form neither adheres to the conventions of classical Perso-Arabic prosody nor follows Nimaic prosody (*'aruz-e Nimai*). This lack of use of metrical structures, whether classical or modern, is widely seen among Iranian critics as a blanket advantage for translators. The "absence of artifice and musicality," the participants concluded, allows Jalali's poetry to move with "ease" from one language to another. It is almost as if the poems just translate themselves. But hey, if the translator is to remain invisible, their invisibility should at least exonerate them from being *traditores*. These critics stopped just short of claiming that Jalali wrote *for* translation. This brings to mind Stephen Owen's famous essay on forms of Chinese poetry that lack tradition and language specificity which made "writing for translation" a hotly debated issue in the 1990s (Owen 1995).

My argument is that these poet-cum-critics —as Owen did after them— conflated poetic effect with poetic practice. Jalali's poetry does not lack artifice, form, or literary adornment. It draws on specific devices—some of which are referenced here—to create the effect of simplicity, straightforwardness, and sincerity. It is crucial to recognize that Jalali does not abandon form but instead moves away from inherited, ready-made formal structures. While his poetics signal change—or radical rupture one must say— to many Persian readers, these same qualities likely become invisible in English translation (depending on which global English readership encounters them), which would lead to obscuring Jalali's distinct style in the source language. Jalali's form is informed, by and large, by incorporating elements of minimalism while eschewing metrical patterns. Persian poetic modernism often marks a break from the regular metrical structures of classical prosody. Whether one defends or critiques this departure, its transformative implications for Persian literary culture are undeniable. Jalali's own reflections capture the stakes of this formal shift:

> Once the foundation of a millennium-old poetic tradition is broken [by virtue] of broken meters and incomplete rhyming patterns, unfortunately, we will witness a type of

destruction that will in all likelihood have disastrous implications. The next stage is to do away with all meters and rhymes: no meter, no rhyme. The following stage is to break sentences with no logical line breaks, or perhaps to place each word on a separate line. Eventually, it may lead to a deaf and dumb story between the poet and his audience and reader. But we will inevitably stage a return. If today we show irreverence by composing free verse, it is because we have no other way. It is justified (2001; 91)

For many English readers, who are quite accustomed to speech rhythms and free verse, Jalali's form may appear as standard or even conservative. However, Adeeba Talukder and I have engaged in earnest with the challenge of preserving his unique poetic qualities. Should these translations fail to exhibit this literary labor, then one can always put up a neon sign that reads: "Caution! Form at Work." Adeeba and I have generated defamiliarize patterns that may otherwise seem automatic to English-speaking readers.

گربهٔ ناخوش
که دستش را می‌لیسد
گوئیا به همه کیهان
فکر می‌کند

و آنچه که همه گربه‌ها
به او گفته‌اند

the ailing cat
who licks her hand
thinks of the entire universe

and what all the other cats
have told her

To approximate the distinctiveness of Jalali's form, we have used several strategies. One approach has been to foreignize the poem's typography, as evident in the poem above which has been justified to the right. This not only disorients the English reader but also slows them down, drawing attention to the poem's structure. A lowercase "i," *à la* E. E. Cummings, reflects both the individualistic voice of Jalali's poetic speaker and its departure from the universal "I." We have adopted a style of enjambment and punctuation more familiar to English readers which differs from Jalali's punctuation-freestyle. On our use of lineation, Adeeba writes,

> In their use of white space, our translation choices are unstraightforward and perhaps might even strike others as unfaithful. In 2012,

when we first translated the poems, our format mirrored Jalali's—in response to his entirely right-justified poems, ours were almost entirely left-justified. However, when we returned to our translations a decade later, we approached the poems with a new poetic sensibility, a renewed sense of the aesthetic, and perhaps a new definition of faithfulness itself. In the end, we have veered away from purely academic translations which map every word in the source language to its closest corresponding word in the target language, because we believe it is an impossible and vain pursuit.

Jalali's work itself is not academic in nature; it eschews the straightforward and goes, as poetry often does, beyond reason. Though Jalali does not employ white space in these poems, he does frequently use enjambment to create a sense of expansiveness around various words, images, and ideas. In these cases, the grammar of Persian rarely ever maps on directly to English grammar, and this sense of capacity cannot be replicated if the format is to be preserved. Our goal, in the end, was to take a poem and create from it another poem; we have aspired not to translate, but to transcreate.

The hope is that these measures will bring dynamic aspects of Jalali's poetics to the surface in English. The following poem reflects some of these decisions and illustrate our efforts to preserve the unique qualities of Jalali's short poems in translation:

بر درخت جهان
مرغ افسانهٔ کلام
نشسته است
و در نگاهش و در فریادش
جهان را روشن‌تر
می‌بینم

on the tree of the world
the mythical
      bird of words
                    sits

& in her wide-eyed gaze
      in her cry

i see the world
      brighter

No translation is the outcome of an unproblematic and total transmission of words and meanings. Elsewhere, I have problematized the idea of untranslatability, arguing that it is rooted in cultural singularity —and romantic nationalism more generally— yet I had thus far overlooked the idea —or the presumption— of translatability. Both concepts have something in common even though they stand for opposite qualities: they serve as floating signifiers. In this case, the misguided idea that Jalali's poetry lacks form and artifice, becomes a statement of fact —as opposed to an argumentative observation— through an unproven and evidenceless argument about translation.

The notion that Jalali's poems move effortlessly into any language fails to account for the creative labor of translation as well as navigating a host of incommensurabilities across two (or more) different literary cultures. In this case, consider the reception of Jalali's work in the source language—going from being derided as disengaged and apolitical to being rediscovered and celebrated for precisely the same qualities previously used to dismiss his poems. It turns out, the very fervor that acted as winds in the sails of literary commitment eventually sank it as a discourse (and practice). Love seemed easy at first, then came the disenchantment of ideology.

As previously noted, some of Jalali's defining poetic qualities—such as enjambment, the absence of punctuation, and his direct, unembellished voice—are necessarily mediated by the conventions and history of non-metrical short poems in English. While some readers may take issue with certain strategies employed here to preserve Jalali's Persian poetics in English, these efforts should move us beyond nebulous and blanket claims of translatability. The big advantage of a bilingual edition is that the words Bijan Jalali composed appear next to the translation. The next section returns us to Jalali's social and literary milieu to explore how was (mis)read and why he has reemerged as a celebrated poet.

Politics of Literary Commitment

The circle of poets affiliated with Nima in the 1950s through the 1970s circulated and popularized his vision of poetic modernism and actively participated in the formation of a modern poetic canon. This circle included Ahmad Shamlu, Mehdi Akhavan-Sales (d. 1990), Forugh Farrokhzad (d. 1967), Reza Baraheni (b. 1935), and a few others. Understanding the role of these figures not just as poets but also as critics and anthologists—or, broadly put, canon-makers—who formed an interpretive culture is integral to the project of poetic modernism in Iran. This perspective helps explain why poets like Jalali were often overlooked or dismissed during this period (although the next section will show that there were exceptions to this rule as well).

Recasting Persian Poetry examines how poets like Akhavan-Sales and Ehsan Tabari (d. 1989) formulated Nima's oeuvre into a coherent poetic discourse of change. Nima's innovations changed the visual appearance, prosodic structures, and sonic landscape of Persian poetry. He departed from the prosodic system of classical forms and introduced lines of varying lengths as well as sporadic rhyming patterns. Karimi-Hakkak writes,

> In time, the discourse solidified into the specific sociolect of the modern voices which emerged in the 1950s and early 1960s and which sought to legitimate the tradition of she'r-e now with sociopolitical interpretations of literary texts. Thus, a whole new interpretive culture emerged wherein poetry was read primarily with the purpose of deciphering the poet's political views, its abstractions and ambiguities attributed to a perennial case of absence of freedoms, particularly those relating to free expression of ideas through poetry (1995; 235)

The emergence of this poetic cohort and its insistence on placing the poetic text within its social context is seen as one of the hallmarks of poetic modernism in the 1960s and 1970s in Iran. The figure of the poet undergoes major changes in modernity: the "wise [man] of the tribe dispensing moral advice and pointing to the path of worldly happiness and salvation" gives way to poet as the voice of his era. New social criteria took form for the modern poet, framed around the aesthetics of commitment.

Baraheni's *Gold in Copper*, a seminal study of modern poetics published in 1968, played a key role in solidifying the discourse of commitment in Iran. Baraheni's introduction, entitled "Today's poet and critic," does not begin with Nima or any other modern figure, Persian or international. He writes: "The poet of our era, ladies and gentlemen of today, must never lose sight of the corpse of Ferdowsi, that farmer of Tus, as it was leaving the gates of Rezan a thousand years ago." The critic alludes to a apocryphal story about Ferdowsi being denied a burial site in his own land by the Ghaznavid monarch.

This story's veracity is not important here. Why does Baraheni begin his manifesto with Ferdowsi's marginalization? From Ferdowsi to Hasanak the Vizier to Mas'ud Sa'd Salman to Amir Kabir, Baraheni forges a unique and selective lineage for the committed poet to hark back to. Behind every valorized poet stands one who has been disowned. And Shamlu's "A Poetry That Is Life," from his 1957 collection *Fresh air*, presents poets who were cast aside. The poem's first stanza, translated by Samad Alavi, professes the modern crisis of Persian poetry as imagined by a committed poet:

موضوع شعر شاعر پیشین
از زندگی نبود.
در آسمان خشک خیالش، او
جز با شراب و یار نمی‌کرد گفتگو

او در خیال بود شب و روز
در دام گیس مضحک معشوقه پای‌بند
حال آنکه دیگران
دستی به جام باده و دستی به زلف یار
مستانه در زمین خدا نعره می‌زنند

    The matter of poetry
    for the bygone poet
    was not life.
    In the barren expanses of his fancy
    he was in dialogue
    only with wine and the beloved.
    Morning and night he was lost in whim,
    seized in the ludicrous snare of his beloved's locks,
    while others
    one hand on the wine cup
    the other on beloved's tresses
    would raise a drunken cry from God's earth.

Creating a poetic lineage was key to modernism and the rise of committed art. *Gold in Copper* helped shape this vision, pushing for criticism that addressed the pressing issues of its time. Baraheni dismissed "art for art's sake" as a betrayal of human suffering and urged writers to engage with the realities around them. Yet, he also believed poetry shouldn't sacrifice beauty for a message—it had to balance artistic power with social purpose. For Baraheni, artists needed to experience life on the streets, where history and society come alive. He grouped creators into three types: detached idealists, oppressive elites, and socially engaged voices who take responsibility for their time.

Yet, Baraheni's criticism wasn't always consistent. While he praised Forugh Farrokhzad's innovations, he criticized Sohrab Sepehri's poetry as shallow. His shifting focus—sometimes aesthetic, sometimes ideological—reflects the broader diversity in how poets approached commitment. There wasn't one way to be a socially engaged artist. Others, like Yadollah Roya'i, took a different path. Roya'i's *She'r-e hajm* (Poetry of Space) broke away from partisan politics, focusing on poetry as a deeply personal, self-aware act. His movement rejected slogans and rigid frameworks, calling instead for an art that stirs engagement from within. Roya'i argued that true commitment starts with revolutionizing the self, creating poetry that is both conscious and aesthetically daring (Roya'i, 2023).

Figure 1: Jalali at Cafe Shuka in Tehran (Photograph by Peyman Hooshmandzadeh)

Bijan Jalali stood even further apart. Quiet and private, Jalali avoided political involvement and literary cliques. Poets like Jalali and Sepehri didn't fit the era's dominant idea of what modern poetry should be. Their work was overshadowed by louder voices that tied modernism to political engagement. But their quieter, more personal approaches offered alternative paths for modern poetry—paths that were overlooked or dismissed in their time. These tensions reveal how rigid ideas about art and politics can erase other voices. Even so, poets like Jalali and Sepehri left behind a legacy of subtle, thought-provoking work. As we'll see, Forugh Farrokhzad's anthologies captured this spectrum, showing that modernism wasn't a single vision but a rich and varied conversation.

To Write is to Anthologize

> My poems' main substance is my suffering. I believe a true poet must have that substance. I compose poetry for my suffering's sake. Form and words, rhyme and rhythm have always been my tools. I have had to change them so they could align with my suffering and that of others
>
> – Nima Yushij, Iranian Writers' Congress, summer 1946

By the late 1960s, a new generation of Iranian poets who had responded to Nima's groundbreaking innovations had come into their own. This modern wave of Persian poetry aimed to connect with social life while reinterpreting its rich literary heritage. Yet the question of how poetry should engage with society was hotly debated. Was poetry meant for readers or for the poet alone? What role did the poet's voice—or the poetic "I"—play in shaping this new literary identity? While scholars often analyze manifestos to understand these shifts, anthologies receive less attention despite their significant role. Manifestos declare change openly, with a rhetoric of urgency and crisis. Anthologies, on the other hand, work more subtly, selecting and organizing poems to present a cohesive vision, often concealing the editor's hand in the process. Each anthology reflects the context in which it was created, offering a window into the cultural and literary currents of its time.

In her brief but remarkable artistic career, Forugh Farrokhzad made lasting contributions to modern

Persian literature. Between 1955 and 1964, she published four collections of poetry (a fifth appeared posthumously in 1974), directed a profoundly poignant and influential film, *The House Is Black*, and translated works by German and English poets and playwrights into Persian. Among these accomplishments was her compilation of *Az Nima ta b'ad* (*From Nima Onward*), an anthology of contemporary Persian poetry published posthumously in 1968.

This anthology, one of the first to feature what we now consider canonical figures of modern Persian poetry, includes 112 poems by 13 poets, such as Bijan Jalali and Ahmad Shamlu. However, Farrokhzad's role as an anthologist is often overlooked, treated as a minor detail in her career. In the preface, Majid Rawshangar recalls discussing the project with Farrokhzad, who wanted to highlight poets influenced by Nima's innovations. Despite Rawshangar's concerns about potential controversy, Farrokhzad dismissed these worries, confident that criticism was inevitable regardless of their efforts.

The anthologization is a long enduring practice in Persian literary culture. For centuries, poets and scholars engaged in varied acts of compilation, commentary, and canonization. Here are several types of anthologies that gained widespread usage and, in some cases, significant proliferation:

Tazkerah: Commemorative or biographical dictionaries documented life stories, anecdotes, and poetry samples. In premodern times, *tazkerahs* played a crucial role in developing metrics for assessing good poetry and sound rhetoric more broadly. In modernity, they served as a foundation for the modern genre of literary history.

Bayaz: Personal notebooks in which admired poetry, prose, and writings for private use were compiled. It was a tool for study, memorization, and personal reflection, often curated with great care. *Bayaz* often functioned as informal archives and helped preserve lesser-known works.

Kashkul: Lit. dervish's bowl. These were eclectic collections of mystical, literary, and philosophical texts. They were diverse, reflecting the compiler's interests, and often lacked a rigid organizational structure. *Kashkuls* symbolize humility and openness to the divine as well as their compiler's spiritual journey.

Safineh: Lit. arc. Collections of texts, often poetry, religious writings, or scientific treatises, meant to preserve and "carry" knowledge, as implied by the metaphorical meaning of arc. They were at times curated as gifts for patrons.

Moraqqaʿ: Typically included calligraphy, paintings, and poetry. The *muraqqaʿ* represents an intersection of literary, artistic, and spiritual traditions. The term itself is a spiritual metaphor on the act of bringing together fragmented pieces into a harmonious whole—a concept resonant in Sufi thought.

Anthologization is how debates were settled and aesthetic norms were codified. Briefly put, this is how the tradition kept inventing itself. In the 20th century, the anthology exploded in numbers and impact with poets like Marinetti, Pound, and Breton shaping movements through their anthologies. In Persian, too, anthologies proliferated in the twentieth century, including Khal Mohammad Khastah's *Moʿaserin-e sokhanvar* (*Contemporary poets*, 1960) and *Yādi az raftagan* (*Remembering those who have passed*, 1965), published around the same time as Farrokhzad's From Nima Onward. Farrokhzad, well-traveled and invested in literary translation, would have been aware of this international trend.

From Nima Onward entered a dynamic literary scene in the 1960s and 1970s, when poets were actively debating the role of poetry and its relationship to tradition. Some aligned with specific schools of thought, while others, like Farrokhzad, sought a broader, more inclusive vision. *From Nima Onward* brought together a new body of work, showcasing the transformation of Persian poetry since Nima. In so doing, it offered one articulation of poetic modernism that Sonboldel would rightly argue became dominant, eclipsing the plurality of modernisms before and after it. Notably, Farrokhzad's anthology included no commentary or analysis—only the selection of poems themselves. Some sections open with a quote from the featured poet; others begin without any introduction, leaving readers to interpret the works on their own.

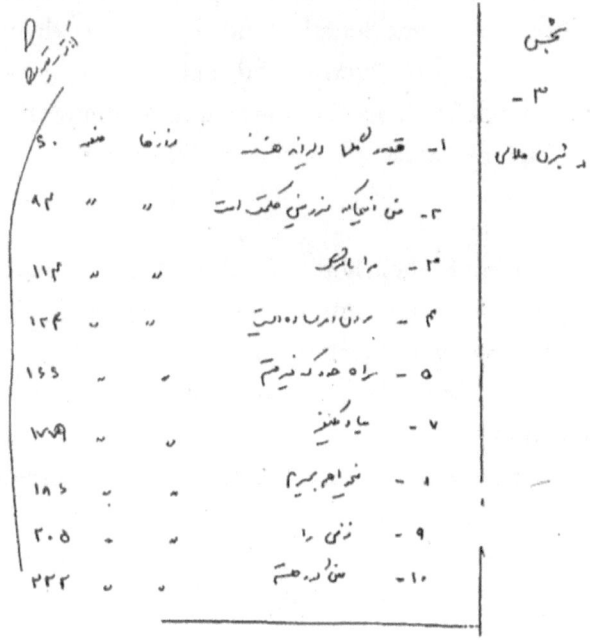

Figure 2: The outline of *From Nima Onward* in Farrokhzad's handwriting

The selection itself reflects Farrokhzad's editorial vision, which sought to mediate between different strands of modern Persian poetry. For example, Shamlu's "A Poetry That Is Life," often viewed as a manifesto for socially engaged poetry, appears alongside Sohrab Sepehri's "Water," which Shamlu had once criticized for lacking any social awareness. Without prior knowledge of these debates, readers encounter the poems on equal footing, free to form their own interpretations. *From Nima to Onward* features various types of free verse—poems with irregular meter, varied line lengths, and little to no rhyme—emphasizing the diversity and innovation of modern Persian poetics. This decision reflects a broader shift in the literary landscape, where form took precedence over content.

Farrokhzad's inclusion of Bijan Jalali should be understood in this context and its social stakes. By the 1990s, this very quality—his refusal to align with dominant ideologies—was re-evaluated as a strength, cementing his place in the modern Persian canon. Farrokhzad not only documented a pivotal moment in Persian poetry but also shaped its future. *From Nima Onward* invited readers to explore a wide spectrum of poetic voices, united by their shared commitment to innovation and modernity. In doing so, she reaffirmed the enduring power of poetry to reflect, challenge, and transform the world around it.

Jalali, After the Dust Settled

> In its frame, the culture will place the portrait of a citizen willing and able to validate or vilify the culture by filtering his or her impressions of it through personal perceptions. To see the events that preoccupy the society registered in poetic works signifies a growing harmony between the poet's role as an individual human being and as a citizen (1995; 134)
>
> —Ahmad Karimi-Hakkak

In modern Persian literature, "representation" and "reflection" have played a key role, viewing literary texts as creative interpretations of the world around us. This perspective emphasizes the social and political responsibilities of literature above all else. While aesthetics and form are considered, the main focus is on how literature engages with the issues of its time. Khorramshahi's earlier analogy— a butterfly net sans butterflies— has subtle undertones of *taʿahhod-e adabi*—literary commitment—where being committed means valuing writing for its power to reflect and respond to the social and political realities of the era.

Between the 1940s and 1970s, Iranian poetry was deeply influenced by the idea of literary commitment—the belief that art should serve a social or political purpose. However, this raised a complex question: who defines what makes art "purposeful"? Despite its popularity, there was no single definition of a committed writer nor was the idea of literary commitment a self-interpreting category. In his influential dissertation, "Poetics of Commitment in Modern Persian," Samad Alavi explores the contradictions and varied expressions of this discourse in both criticism and poetry.

The 1980s shifted the conversation around literary commitment, a concept historically tied to leftist intellectuals in Persian literary circles. The aftermath of the revolution led to widespread disillusionment among many writers. Those who fought against censorship and political isolation were often silenced or forced into exile. During this period, the state-supported *maktabi* literary movement arose, driven by its own ideological goals. In response, figures like Baraheni and Mohammad Mokhtari revisited their earlier convictions and the value judgments generated by them. Baraheni, for example, republished *Gold in Copper* in 1992, omitting the combative introduction publisher in the first edition. Instead, his reflections turned inward, focusing on literature's social role. He later dismissed the poetics of literary commitment entirely in an essay titled "Why I am no longer a Nimaic poet."

It is in this changing landscape that Bijan Jalali is rediscovered by a new generation of readers. By the 1990s, his work attracted more attention than in his entire lifetime. His unpublished poems from the 1970s were released, and he was honored with the Gardun

Literary Award in 1996. This is unsurprising, given how closely the experiential poetics of the 1990s and early 2000s align with Jalali's poetics. His poetry has been translated into multiple languages, and in 2000, Kamyar Abedi published *Zamzameh'i bara-ye abadiyat* (A *whisper for eternity*), a collection of essays written by poets, critics, and friends on Jalali's work. And in 2018, he edited another robust work on the poet, titled *Bijan Jalali, she'r'hayash va del-e ma* (*Bijan Jalali, his poems and our hearts*). Writing this essay would have been quite difficult without Kamyar Abedi's meticulously researched and edited books on the poet. Jalali has also gained more recognition through the establishment of a literary award named in his honor, presented to poets like Simin Behbahani. What makes Jalali's poetic career particularly fascinating is that he received support from conservative modernists such as Behbahani and traditional critics like Khorramshahi, yet he was overlooked by modernists such as Shamlu, who, like Jalali, also experimented with prose poetry.

Perhaps the true measure of Jalali's re-emergence and growing popularity as a poet lies not in the realm of literary criticism, but in music. In 2018, the Kamkars, released the album *Hich dar hich* (*Nothing in nothing*) which draws heavily on Jalali's poetry. The Kamkars are one of the most celebrated and influential musical families in Iran, renowned for their contributions to Kurdish and classical Iranian musical traditions and credit for training newer generations of musicians. In spiritual forms of Islam, "nothingness" represents the annihilation of the ego (*fana*) to achieve spiritual union with the Divine. *Nothing in nothing* then explores existential questions about life, mortality, and the search for meaning.

Figure 3: Cover of the Kamkars' album *Hich dar hich*

The Kamkars had previously put to music verses by Rumi, Hafez, and other classical Persian lyricists. On working with Jalali's poetry, Hushang Kamkar told *Musiqi-ye ma* magazine,

> Modern mysticism [*'erfan-e modern*] is one of the characteristics of Bijan Jalali's poetry. This album, based on its goal of blending and juxtaposing elements of tradition and modernity, has put in dialogue Rumi's

> traditional mysticism with Jalali's modern mysticism through poetic and melodic imagery… [this synthesis] has given the entire work a unified spiritual form. It is a deliberate and innovative endeavor that may attract criticism from traditional-minded people. [Rumi's] hemistich "*Man gholam-e qamaram ghayr-e qamar hich magu* (I am the servant of the moon; speak of nothing but the moon) is heard at the beginning of the work and, repeated like a leitmotif in other segments. It is also heard in the closing measures of the final track, "A Elegy for the Poet," played on the clarinet, whose sound symbolizes death (2018)

The broader context of this reception includes the death of Bijan Elahi in 2010, which sparked a significant wave of rereading avant-garde, Sufi-inspired poetry, largely associated with "Other poetry" movement or *She ʿr-e digar*. This was an entirely non-Nimaic movement that built on the experiments of Moqaddam, Tondar Kia, and Hushang Irani. That Jalali now belongs in the same soundscape shows how poetic (and musical) lineage will always search for and invent the tradition it needs, be it in the mold of commitment, spirituality, or modern spirituality in this case.

I would be remiss not to mention how social media has contributed to popularizing Jalali's verse. One can now speak of a digital genre of visual art, a phenomenon that has redefined how poetry is shared and enjoyed. Jalali's poem lends itself uniquely well to visual art due to its brevity. He is quite popular on Instagram where users have combined his verses with striking images, typography, or minimalistic designs, turning the poem into a visual experience that resonates well beyond the written text.

I don't know how Jalali would have felt about digital receptions of his work given his critical attention to how his words appeared on the white page. The silent spaces on the page were as crucial to the work as the words spilled in ink. Depending on the poem, these spaces invite readers to linger on the infinite, look into the vast field of existence, or meditate on the economy of language. In other poems, these white spaces evoke a sense of boundlessness, mirroring the natural landscapes and cosmic scales his poetry often evokes. Jalali writes of his own work,

> Formal features of both classical and modern verse that have become visual markers of poetry at large are no longer present in my work. My poems depart from poetic conventions; they will surprise those who qualify a poem first and foremost by its external features, in other words as a piece of literature. My writings are less concerned with the concept of literature and the art of poetry,

and more with writing poetry itself. There are many theories on poetry these days that poetry itself has been neglected.

This passage highlights Jalali's quiet revolt, one directed at what he perceives to be the overtheorization and conventionalization of Persian poetry. In this vein, poetry as a highhanded craft could overshadow the raw, emotive, and intuitive aspects of poetic creation. Considering how much Jalali valued the social role of poetry, it feels fitting that his poems have found a place on social media. Visualization of his verse is just another medium among other methods through which Jalali's younger readers intimately converse with his work.

Toward the end of his life, Jalali began to engage more with his audience. He frequented Cafe Shuka in Tehran, where he held long discussions with young literary enthusiasts about poetry. He even had his own special table at the cafe, *miz-e Jalali*. His poetry was once criticized as detached, elitist, and indifferent to social concerns. Today, however, a new generation sees him as a deeply introspective poet, wrongly overlooked and misunderstood by a politically charged climate. Abedi praises Jalali for maintaining an "independent voice," in an era when poetry was tasked with envisioning justice. Jalali's poetry is often viewed in contrasting lights: one generation sees him as a poet disconnected from the socio-political anxieties of his time, while the other reveres him as a timeless figure, whose poems transcend time and place.

My own effort to reframe Jalali within his social and literary context—highlighting his marginalized modernist poetics—is also a selective interpretation of his work. I hope it encourages a deeper consideration of his poetry as part of the larger history of Persian poetic modernism. Though this essay has minimized biographical details, it's worth asking: Who was Bijan Jalali the individual? His friends describe him as gentle, humble, and the very embodiment of his poetry.

Jalali's deep connection to animals was an important side of his personality. He lived with dogs and cats and was a devoted animal lover. Jalali's friends remember how he would always feed stray cats and dogs and feel deeply offended when friends called them ugly. "I hold a reverent, almost religious respect for life, and to me, plants and animals—the purest forms of life—are sacred," Jalali once told fellow poet Ahmad Reza Ahmadi (1994; 126-127). The literary translator Goli Emami, who first encouraged me to work on Jalali's poetry, shared with me, "If you met him and didn't know he was a poet, you would never guess. He never talked about his poetry, but always engaged in deep conversations about a wide range of topics." He never married and after his passing, his brother and nephew continued to promote his work. Jalali fell into a coma in December 1999, never to see the new millennium.

Amelia Ossorio's beautiful and whimsical design on this book's cover celebrates Jalali's life in the company of his house plants and animal friends.

و روزی خواهند گفت
که یکی بود – یکی نبود
یک شاعری بود
به نام بیژن جلالی
که شعر سفید می‌گفت
و حالا ما یادمان رفته
که او چه می‌گفت
و فقط یک سطر
یک کلمه یک حرف
از شعر او برای ما
باقی مانده است

And one day they will say
once upon a time,

there was a poet
    named Bijan Jalali

who recited free verse

and now our memory of
    what it was

he said

escapes us
save for

a single word, one letter
of his poetry
    that for us

perseveres

Aria Fani
Seattle,
2016-2025

Bijan Jalali's oeuvre

Ruz'ha [Days]. Morvarid, 1962.
Del-e ma va jahan [Our hearts and the world]. Morvarid, 1965.
Rang-e ab'ha [The color of waters]. Self-published, Nil, 1971.
Ab va aftab [Water and sun]. Ruz, 1983.
Bazi-ye nur [The play of light]. Navid, 1990.
Ruzaneh'ha [Dailies]. Farzan Ruz, 1995.
Darbareh-e she'r [On poetry]. Self-published, Farzan, 1998.
Didar'ha [Encounters]. Morvarid, 2001.
Naqsh-e jahan [Image of the world]. Morvarid, 2001.
She'r-e sokut [The verse of silence]. Morvarid, 2002.
She'r-e khak, she'r-e khurshid [Poetry of the soil, poetry of the sun]. Morvarid, 2003.
She'r-e payan, she'r-e duri [Poetry of the end, poetry of separation]. Morvarid, 2004.

References

Abedi, Kamyar. *Zamzamehi bara-ye abadiyat: Bijan Jalali, She'rhayash va del-e ma [Whispers for Eternity]*. Tehran: Nashr-e Ketab-e Nader, 2000.

Ahmadi, Ahmad Reza. "Goftogu ba Bijan Jalali." *Kelk* 34 (1992).

Ahmed, Amr Taher. *La Révolution Littéraire: Étude de L'influence de la Poésie Française sur la Modernisation des Formes Poétiques Persanes au Début du Xxe Siècle*. Wien: Verlag der Österreichischen Akademie der Wissenschaften, ÖAW, 2012.

Alavi, Samad. "The Poetics of Commitment in Modern Persian: A Case of Three Revolutionary Poets in Iran." PhD diss., University of California, Berkeley, 2014.

Baraheni, Reza. *Tala dar mes: Dar she'r va sha'eri*. Tehran: Zaman, 1968.

Baraheni, Reza. *Tala dar mes: Dar she'r va sha'eri*. 3 vols. Tehran: Nevisandeh, 1992.

Baraheni, Reza. *Khata beh parvanah'ha: She'r, va: Chera man digar sha'ir-e Nima'i nistam: Bahsi dar Sha'eri*. Tehran: Markaz, 1995.

Baraheni, Reza, and Nasir Hariri. "Goft va shenudi ba Ahmad Shamlu." In *Honar va adabiyat-e emruz*. Tehran: Ketabsara-ye babul, 1365/1986.

Behbahani, Simin. "Bijan Jalali, sha'eri ke az gham kam goft." *Payam-e hamun*. Esfand 23, 1378 / March 13, 2000.

Brookshaw, Dominic P, and Nasrin Rahimieh. *Poet of Modern Iran*. London: I. B. Tauris, 2010.

Cavanagh, Clare, Stephen Cushman, Roland Greene, Jahan Ramazani, and Paul Rouzer. *The Princeton Encyclopedia of Poetry and Poetics*. Princeton, N.J: Princeton University Press, 2012.

Emami, Karim, and Hura Yavari. *Karim Emami on Modern Iranian Culture, Literature & Art*. New York: Persian Heritage Foundation, 2014.

Fallah, Mehrdad, "Va chenin shod ke sha'er az aseman beh khiyaban qadam gozasht," *Farhang-e towse'eh*, no. 49 (May 2001): 10.

Fani, Aria. "The Allure of Untranslatability: Shafi'i-Kadkani and (Not) Translating Persian Poetry." *Iranian Studies*. 2021, 54(1-2): 95-125.

Farrokhzad, Forugh. *Daftarha-ye zamaneh*. 1355/1976.

Farrukhzad, Forugh, and Majid Rawshangar. *Az Nima ta ba'd: Bargozidehi az she'r-e emruz-e Iran*. Tehran: Morvarid, 1968.

Friedman, Susan Stanford. *Planetary Modernisms: Provocations on Modernity Across Time*. Columbia University Press, 2015.

Hafiz, and Ahmad Shamlu. *Hafiz-e Shiraz: Beh revayat-e Shamlu*. Tehran: Entesharat-e Morvarid, 1976.

Ingenito, Domenico. *Beholding Beauty: Sa'di of Shiraz and the Aesthetics of Desire in Medieval Persian Poetry*. Brill, 2020.

Janecek, J. Gerald. "Minimalism in Contemporary Russian Poetry: Vsevolod, Nekrasov and Others." *The Slavonic and East European Review* 70, no. 3 (1992): 401–419.

Kadkani, Shafi'i. "Estelah-e she'r-e azad va she'r-e sepid." In *Ba cheragh va ayineh*, 277–83. Tehran: Sokhan, 2011.

Karimi-Hakkak, Ahmad. *Recasting Persian Poetry: Scenarios of Poetic Modernism in Iran*. Salt Lake City: University of Utah Press, 1995.

Karimi-Hakkak, Ahmad. *An Anthology of Modern Persian Poetry*. Boulder, CO: Westview Press, 1994.

Karimi-Hakkak, Ahmad, and Kamran Talattof. *Essays on Nima Yushij: Animating Modernism in Persian Poetry*, edited by Ahmad Karimi-Hakkak and Kamran Talattof, 221–235. Leiden: Brill, 2004.

Khorrami, Mehdi. *Literary Subterfuge and Contemporary Persian Fiction: Who Writes Iran?* London: Routledge, 2015.

Khorramshahi, Baha' al-Din. "Jalal dar She'r-e Jalali." In *Nabz-e she'r: Majmu'eh-i naqd-e she'r bar hejdah sha''r, az Shamlu ta Hiva Masih*, 403–6. Tehran: Rawshan-e Mehr, 2004.

Kianush, Mahmud. *Modern Persian Poetry*. Ware: Rockingham Press, 1996.

Shamlu, Ahmad. *Mafahim-e rend va rendi dar ghazal-e Hafez*. San Jose, CA: Nashr-e Zamanah, 1991.

Mohit, Ahmad. *The World is My Home*. Tehran: Agah, 2007.

Musiqi-ye ma. "The latest work by Hoshang Kamkar was inspired by the poetry of Bijan Jalali," May 16, 2018. Accessed December 23, 2024.
https://www.musicema.com/node/348706

Owen, Stephen. "What Is World Poetry?" Critical Terms for Literary Study, edited by Frank Lentricchia and Thomas McLaughlin, 2nd ed., University of Chicago Press, 1995, pp. 325-346.

Roya'i, Yadollah. *Az sakku-ye sorkh: Masa'il-e she'r.* Tehran: Entesharat-e Morvarid, 1978.

Roya'i, Yadollah. *'Ebarat as chis: Masa'el-e she'r.* Tehran: Entesharat-e Negah, 2023.

Sepehri, Sohrab, and Karim Emami. *The Lover Is Always Alone.* Tehran: Sokhan Publishers, 2004.

Shamlu, Ahmad. *On Different Aspects of Persian Literary Culture.* Berkeley: University of California, Public lecture, April 1991.

"Shaʿer-e sheʿr-e sokut: Goftogu ba Ahmad Reza Ahmadi." *Negah-e no* 22 (Mehr 1373/October 1994).

Smith, Matthew C. "Literary Courage: Language, Land and the Nation in the Works of Malik al-Shuʿara Bahar." PhD diss., Harvard University, 2006.

Sonboldel, Farshad. *The Rebellion of Forms in Modern Persian Poetry: Politics of Poetic Experimentation.* Bloomsbury, 2024

Sonboldel, Farshad. "Dismantling the Poetic Father: An Antithetical Reading of Nimaic Poetry in the 1370s/1990s and 1380s/2000s: Case Studies of Ātifah Chahārmahāliyān and Pigāh Ahmadī." *Encyclopaedia Iranica.* Last updated November 20, 2024. https://poets.iranicaonline.org/article/dismantling-the-poetic-father-an-antithetical-reading-of-nimaic-poetry-in-the-1370s-1990s-and-1380s-2000s-case-studies-of-atifah-chaharmahaliyan-and-pigah-ahmadi/.

Tikku, Girdhari L., and Alireza Anushiravani. *A Conversation with Modern Persian Poets.* Costa Mesa, CA: Mazda Publishers, 2004.

Thompson, Levi. *Reorienting Modernism in Arabic and Persian Poetry.* Cambridge University Press, 2022.

Zavarzadeh, Masʿud. "Abandonment is Theme of Jalali's Free Verse." In *Critical Perspectives on Modern Persian Literature*, edited by Thomas M. Ricks, 438–41. Washington, D.C.: Three Continents Press, 1984.

Acknowledgements

It all started with Goli Emami, as often happens in Aria's life. In 2010, she mailed Aria a few collections of Bijan Jalali's poems, encouraging him to delve deeper into modern Persian poetry beyond its most celebrated figures. This journey would not have been possible without the support of so many in our community of practice: Robert Alter, Chana Kronfeld, Wali Ahmadi, Samad Alavi, Ahmad Karimi-Hakkak, Kevin Schwartz, Mehdi Khorrami, Bristin Jones, Kamyar Abedi, Niloufar Talebi, Shadab Zeest Hashmi and Faisal Mohyuddin. In more recent years, Caro Reed-Ferrara, Anna Learn, and Farshad Sonboldel have been immensely supportive of this project.

We owe special gratitude to Mahdi Ganjavi of Asemana Books, who has provided a perfect home for Jalali's arrival in English. A number of poems have previously appeared in the following publications: PBS Frontline, Poetry International, Shahadat, Waxwing Magazine, Green Linden Press. The essay, "In Quiet Revolt," is a revised version of the following publication, reprinted here with permission: Aria Fani, "A Silent Conversation with Literary History: Re-theorizing Modernism in the Poetry of Bijan Jalali," *Iranian Studies* 50, no. 4 (2017): 523–552. Anna Learn, Sam Hodgkin, and Farshad Sonboldel provided valuable critical feedback on the revised drafts of this article.

Behind the words & images

Bijan Jalali (1927–1999) was an Iranian poet known for his brief, minimalist, meditative style. Departing from traditional Persian verse, his poems focus on the nature of poetic production, the cosmos, and nature. Though overlooked during his lifetime, Jalali's work has gained posthumous recognition for its quiet yet profound impact on modern Persian poetry.

Adeeba Shahid Talukder is a Pakistani and Bengali-American poet, vocalist, and translator of Urdu and Persian poetry. She is the author of *Shahr-e-jaanaan: The City of the Beloved* (Tupelo Press, 2020), winner of the 2017 Kundiman Poetry Prize, and the chapbook *What Is Not Beautiful* (Glass Poetry Press, 2018). Her work has appeared in *Washington Square Review, Gulf Coast, World Literature Today, Aleph Review, The Margins, Words Without Borders*, and various other publications. Adeeba holds an MFA in Creative Writing from the University of Michigan and has received fellowships from Kundiman and Poets House. She is currently training in Hindustani classical music under Ustad Salamat Ali and is the recipient of a grant from the New York State Council on the Arts.

Aria Fani is an assistant professor of Persian and Iranian studies at the University of Washington, where he co-convenes the Translation Studies Hub. His first book, *Reading across Borders: Afghans, Iranians, and Literary Nationalism* is available in both English (University of Texas Press, 2024), and Persian (Shirazeh Press, 2024). Outside of academia, he advocates for non-citizen Americans, focusing on asylum seekers from Central America.

Domenico Ingenito, Associate Professor of Iranian Studies at UCLA, specializes in premodern Persian literature, visual culture, and gender studies. His interdisciplinary research integrates philology, literary theory, and manuscript studies, focusing on Persian lyricism. His notable works include *Beholding Beauty: Saʿdi of Shiraz and the Aesthetics of Desire in Medieval Persian Poetry* (Brill, 2020) and the critical edition and Italian translation of Forugh Farrokhzad's collected poems, *Io parlo dai confini della notte: tutte le poesie* (Bompiani, 2023).

Amelia Ossorio is an illustrator from Seattle who creates vibrant and playful designs that invite curiosity and nostalgia. She studies Persian at the University of Washington's Middle Eastern Languages and Cultures department and is one of Aria Fani's students. Her work draws inspiration from a wide range of contemporary artists that emphasize self-reflection and freedom, including Forugh Farrokhzad and Frida Kahlo. She often incorporates symbols from nature, colorful scenes from life, and memories into her illustrations. Ossorio's art can be found online under the name @sensitive.cactus.

Asemana Books

Devoted to Publishing Diasporic, Underrepresented and Progressive Literature on the Middle East.

Email: Asemanabooks@gmail.com

Webpage: asemanabooks.ca

Scholarly and Academic Research

- *Tanglusha of a Thousand Images: Essays on Culture and Literature* – Reza Farokhfal – 2024
- *Language, People, and Society: Iranian Minority Languages and Literary Traditions* – Edited by Amir Kalan, Mahdi Ganjavi, Anisa Jafari, Lale Javanshir – 2024
- *Music on the Borderland: Remembering and Chronicling the 1979 Revolution's Shadow on Iranian Music* – Keyan Emami – 2024
- *Implications of Class Analysis in Capitalist Imperialism* – Mohammad Hajinia and Shahrzad Mojab – 2024
- *Dark Night and Phoenixes of the Ashes: Nima Yushij's Poetry from 1932–1942* – Ramin Ahmadi – 2024
- *Whispers of Oasis: Likoo's Poetic Mirage* – Mahdi Ganjavi, Amin Fatemi, Mansour Alimoradi – 2024
- *Hafez and Irony* – Reza Farokhfal – 2024
- *Kurdish Women at the Core of the Historical Contradictions on Feminism and Nationalism* – Shahrzad Mojab – 2023

- *The Peasant Uprising of Mukriyan 1952–1953: Consulate Documents, Diplomatic Correspondence, and the Press Coverage* – Amir Hassanpour – 2022

Critical Edition

- *The History of Changes in Iran* – Mirza Agha Khan Kermani, edited by M. Rezaei Tazik – 2024
- *Rostam in the Twenty-Second Century* – Abdulhussain San'atizadeh Kermani, edited by Mahdi Ganjavi and M. Mansouri – 2017

Poetry

- *One Hundred Nights of Yearning* – Mansour Noorbakhsh – 2025
- *Songs of Barbad* – Amir Hakimi – 2024
- *With My Shadows, I Created Myself* – Hadi Ebrahimi Roudbaraki
- *Citizens of September* – Saeid Rezadoust
- *Wonder of Memory* – Amir Hakimi – 2023
- *Galaxy Has No Memory of the Sunset* – Mahdi Ganjavi – 2023
- *Strangers Who Live in Me* – Mahdi Ganjavi – 2021
- *Exiled to the Rocky* – Ali Fatolahi – 2018

Fiction & Plays

- *An Iranian Odyssey* – Rana Soleimani – 2025
- *Lead to Evil* – Javad Alavi – 2025

- *We Are Drunk and Broken, and No One Is Witnessing Us* – Mahdi Ganjavi – 2025
- *Someone Had Died in Front of Our House* – Akbar Falahzadeh – 2024
- *Zinat* – Vahid Zarrabi Nasab – 2024
- *Siberian Crane* – Ali Foumani
- *Elephants Reached the Plain* – Kaveh Oveisi
- *Textual Mosaic* – Marzieh Sotoudeh – 2024
- *Expectations of a Dream* – Mahdi Ganjavi – 2020

Asemana Books is devoted to publishing diasporic, underrepresented, and progressive literature on the Middle East.

asemanabooks.ca

ASEMANA BOOKS

www.ingramcontent.com/pod-product-compliance
Lightning Source LLC
Chambersburg PA
CBHW030853170426
43193CB00009BA/597